Bette writes straight fr — the
Lord.

Carol M. Byrd
Retired English Teacher & Instructor

Bette has a great sense of humor and a deep compassion for the human element as reflected in her poem, "The Vacancy" which brought me to tears. You will find Bette an excellent writer and a kind and compassionate friend.

Ruth C. Ellinger
Award-Winning Author

Bette Lafferty is one of my all-time favorite poets and this latest book is a treasure! As one of her Monday Morning Offerings recipients for the last two years, I can attest to how many times the poems arriving in my inbox made me smile, reminisce or think a little deeper. Her talent for description that makes readers visualize each scenario is one I wish were mine. Step into Bette's world and experience the love that has brought her true peace and contentment. It's a purchase you won't regret!

Cheryl Johnston
Word Weavers Tampa
National League of American Pen Women

Bette's words reveal an extraordinary woman who has faced and prevailed over large and small circumstances of life. Her resilience and positivity will encourage you to keep expecting God to meet you wherever you are.

Barbara Routen
FOCUS Magazine - staff writer
National League of American Pen Women
Letters and Music member

A lovely way to start the day from one of my fave people! Bette wrote her way into my heart years ago; I'm one of her biggest fans. I know this little book will become your go-to for inspiration.

Debora M. Coty
Award-winning author of over 40 books,
including the bestselling
Too Blessed to be Stressed series.

CONTENTS

ACKNOWLEDGMENTS

I write to the glory of the Lord and thank Him for the gift of writing that He has given me.

I thank my husband for buying and teaching me the computer

I thank good friend Patsy Hink who has been my encourager for almost 50 years

I thank my friend Annie Morgan who tried to teach me the fundamentals of English

I thank my friend Chris Ritter for checking my work and for being a cheerleader for years

I thank Carol Byrd for believing in me and teaching me the basics of life story writing

I thank Val Perry for her guidance and encouragement in my writing life stories

I thank Cheryl Johnson, Debbie Coty and Ruth Carmicle Ellinger for sharing their knowledge and

wisdom regarding what makes a good writer and for traversing the winding roads to having my

work published.

And many, many more…

1 All in Fun

I try to remember
What was done,
All in the name
Of having fun.

There were marbles, hopscotch
And jumping rope too,
Kick-the-can,
So much to do.

Sand boxes full
Of castles so tall,
We were just children,
But we had it all.

There were paintbrushes,
Chalk and crayons galore,
So much fun,
Who could want for more?

Cherry trees to climb
While the pears would fall,
We were just children,
But we had it all.

Tricycles to ride
And roller-skates too,
Sled rides and ice skates,
So much to do.

Swings and sliding boards,
Cart wheels and games,
The reading of books
That left you never the same.

The playing of dress-up
And a high heel shoe,
A world of make-believe,
So much to do.

We each had a doll
When we were small,

Having fun as children,

We had it all.

2 Heavenly Cords

The music of heaven,

Unknown to man,

Has notes like songbirds

After a storm,

Powerful yet soothing,

Exhilarating yet peaceful,

Engulfing every sense

God created in man,

Amplified.

The silence between notes

Echoes beyond magnificent,

Kindled by God's Spirit,

Are sweeter,

Joy filled,

Life giving and

Beyond belief.

A gift of grace

All to God's Glory.

Who, but God,

Creator of breath,

Gives to His children,

Once dead, now alive,

Such spectacular garments

Of vibrant colored sound

Pulsating through

A body new in Christ.

Only God, our Father,

Maker of heaven and earth,

Is capable of creating

All beauty

To perfection.

Before time began,

He fingered the notes

And filled the heavens

With His voice of love called music.

3 Friends to the Rescue

The realization that I might have talent as a writer is incredible. How could that be, me of all people? I'm a poor speller, a slow reader, and have a memory like a sieve. As far as I'm concerned, these are not the qualities possessed by great writers. Yet my friends continue to encourage me to write.

"Organize your desk," they say. "Assemble what you have already written. Don't let self-doubt hold you back. Submit some of your poetry. What have you to lose?" Having buckled under the pressure, I've agreed to try, but finding the time to do all that they suggest has become another stumbling block. My daily appointment book is already crammed full.

"You don't find time to write," my friends quickly point out. "You make time to write." Much to my surprise, I have been able to do this. The results are a pile of neatly typed poems with no place to go.

Enter my friends again, to the rescue. "Try the library!" they suggest.

Why hadn't I thought of that? Friends can be so helpful, but I must admit they seem a little impatient with me these days. The librarian directed me to a variety of books that hold unlimited possibilities. Success seems possible, but the idea of actually sending my writings to someone is a little scary. The little voice in the back of my head agrees with me, too.

"You're nobody," it says. "Why would any editor want to read your work?" Then procrastination attacks with a vengeance. I couldn't even type the envelopes or lick the stamps.

My friends plead with me again. "You've come so far, why stop now? Just send them."

Somehow, I have become locked on pause. Days come and go; I avoid my office like the plague. My scheduled writing time vanishes. I've begun to question myself again. Perhaps the little voice in my head is right. Maybe I should stick to gardening. I'm good at that. Then another voice speaks, "O ye of little faith. It was not your idea to write, it was mine. I've called you to do this work. You are not alone. Don't you understand?"

The voice continued, "Don't be so shocked that you didn't seek my help. You are no different from the others whom I have chosen. Remember Peter? He feared for his life. You only fear receiving rejection letters. Trust Me, when rejection comes, we'll handle it together." These thoughts dazed me. It was like taking an ice-cold shower. Once you get past the shock, you are definitely awake and ready for anything. Therefore, I'm happy to announce that I finally mailed my first batch of envelopes. My friends are ecstatic. I just pray that when I start receiving those intimidating rejection letters, I'll be ready. Perhaps, I'll just forward them to my friends. After all, they've earned them.

"I lift up my eyes to the mountains — where does my help come from? My help comes from the LORD."

Psalm 121:1–2 NIV

4 Why I Write

What is the purpose of all these words,
when so much has already been said?
What is the reason, why add more
to the volumes already unread?

I question my motive, is it worth my time
for the sleepless nights devoted to rhyme?
What of the cost of paper and ink,
if my words don't matter or cause you to think?

What could I say that's possibly new,
to catch your attention, to encourage you?
Why should I bother to rack my brain
if all you want is to remain the same?

We all know words are powerful indeed.
They're able to motivate us, if we please.
But it only takes a stubborn heart
to keep us from becoming really smart.

While some words make music that entertain;
others come as warnings of heavy rain.
Some words bring stories of war on earth,
but, the most powerful tell of Jesus' birth.

So, my purpose is simple, I'm happy to say,
my words just keep coming both night and day.
When my brain turns on, I'll no longer fight.
I'll let them keep coming and continue to write.

5 An Offering of Love

May we ever grow in wisdom,

May we ever praise God's name,

As we search His Word for meaning,

May we never be the same.

May God's love explode within us,

Then flow with perfect ease,

To others be it given,

As our offering – may it please.

In a world whose heart is troubled,

May it find in us a friend,

As we gladly share Christ Jesus,

And His love, which has no end.

6 Speak Up

Fear is often said to be the path leading to failure. Unfortunately, I have traveled down more than my fair share of those trails. Luckily, I have learned many valuable lessons trudging through the swamps of life. One such experience that remains clearly etched in my memory raised its ugly head during my first real job the summer I turned fifteen.

The owner of a small coffee shop hired me as a waitress. Four small tables were available for guests while eight stools stood at attention at a lunch counter. I was terribly nervous but confident I could manage. How hard could that be, I asked myself, only breakfast and lunch were served. It didn't take me long to find out.

"Your job will be to take orders, cook, do dishes, sweep the floor, and anything else that needs to be done," the owner said, barely looking up from his desk. "In turn,

I'll pay you seventy-five cents an hour. I'll expect you to be on time, too, young lady."

"Yes sir," I whispered, hoping he didn't notice my trembling legs. "Thank you, sir," I mumbled as I spun on my heels and quickly exited his office.

Seventy-five cents was the minimum hourly wage back in 1951 and three times as much as I made babysitting. I could see dollars stuffing my pockets; by the end of the summer, I figured I'd be rich.

But first, there were two definite problems I had to address. The coffee shop was located in downtown Toledo, about a thirty-minute drive from my home. Not being a morning person, that meant crawling out of bed early, getting dressed and out the door before my brain kicked into gear. Next, came a half-mile walk to the bus stop, riding into town alone, and then walking several more blocks to get to work. This country girl had never been to town before all alone. With low blood pressure,

I moved more like a turtle than a jogger. And second, I didn't know how to cook.

I arrived early on my first day of work with a stomach full of butterflies. The owner, turned out to be a kind old gentleman. He immediately began showing me my duties. I knew how to wash dishes, and the cleaning chores came naturally. But when he showed me the menu and started explaining where things were, it put the fear of God in me. My mother never taught me anything about cooking. I knew I'd mess up and get fired. I bluffed my way through his instructions and prayed like crazy.

Finally, the bewitching hour arrived and the doors were unlocked. People began strolling in for breakfast.

"Orange juice, please."

"Coffee and toast, honey."

So far, so good, I thought. Then a tall, friendly policeman came in and ordered a milkshake with a raw egg. I couldn't imagine putting a slimy egg into a tasty chocolate shake, so I questioned him about the idea. He guaranteed me that he drank one here every morning, and I shouldn't let it worry my pretty little head.

The next customer ordered coffee, toast, scrambled eggs, and bacon. I smiled and walked slowly to the grill. Popping the bread into the toaster, my brain did cartwheels trying to imagine how to scramble an egg. I stood staring at the hot grill just as another waitress clocked in.

"Hi," she said. "You must be the new girl."

"Yes," I replied.

After a couple moments of small talk, I sadly confessed to her my dilemma.

"No problem," she whispered, "I'll handle them. It'll be our secret."

She was so kind. Whenever I drew a blank, she was right there to help me. She explained how to fry a hamburger, roll a hot dog, clean the grill, and set up for the next morning. She was my guardian angel, quieting all my fears. I began to truly enjoy working at the coffee shop. Several weeks passed without any incidents.

Then one day, I arrived earlier than usual. As I opened the back door to the coffee shop, there sat Jake, the man who squeezed our orange juice. We were both startled to see each other. As I stared at him, I recalled the words of warning from the other waitresses.

"He's a poor excuse for a man," they said. "Be careful. Why the boss ever hired him is a mystery to us."

His hair was shaggy and matted; he was unshaven, and his clothes were soiled and unkempt. My nose detected that he needed a good bath, too.

"Oh! Good morning," I finally managed to say.

He just glared at me and grunted. Then, it happened. Horror upon horror, as he squeezed the juice, he spit chewing tobacco into the container.

"What are you doing?"

"Never you mind," he snarled as he stood up. "And you best not tell anyone what you have seen or I'll report you to the authorities. You're working here illegally. You're only fifteen, and I know that you don't have a worker's permit. I'll get the cops to put you in jail, little girl."

Fear gripped my throat like a vice as he stood there hovering over me. I was so frightened; I didn't know what to say. I didn't want to go to jail. What was I to do? My legs felt like gelatin as they struggled to carry me into the front of the shop. I strained to catch my breath as I prepared the grill for the day.

When my regular customers arrived, I steered them away from the orange juice, making stupid excuses why they shouldn't order it. The tension created a fierce headache. I dropped a cup, spilled coffee, and finally decided that seventy-five cents an hour just wasn't worth ending up in jail. At the end of my shift, I went to the owner and told him that I had to quit.

"I'm sorry, but it just isn't working out with my schedule," I lied.

He said that he was sorry too. He sat down at his desk and wrote out my paycheck. I thanked him and rushed out of his office. I couldn't get out of that place fast enough.

The ride home seemed to take forever. I felt awful, so ashamed, and such a failure. I anguished over what I'd tell my parents. My dad would probably yell at me, but telling him a lie would hurt less than his condemnation.

Fear's crippling power kept me a slave until my mid-thirties, at which time I invited the Lord into my life. He soon replaced my fear with faith in Him. When I began to write my life stories in my late sixties, I realized I had never told my parents the truth about the incident. My father had died by then, but my mother was surprised to learn what had really happened.

"The shop has long closed its doors," she said. "I wonder if Jake's secret was ever revealed."

"I guess we will never know, Mother."

Thank goodness, with the help of God, fear no longer defines who I am. And armed with His truth, time has become my friend as I've traveled over the many bumpy roads in my life. I realize one incident doesn't make me a failure. One lie, although not God pleasing, doesn't set my path in stone. Forgiveness has made me stronger.

Yet, somewhere in the back chambers of my mind, I can still see and sense the fear of my encounter with Jake.

Submit yourselves, then, to God.
Resist the devil, and he will flee from you.
James 4:7 NIV

7 Capturing a Dream

Where do dreams come from?

How do they actually start?

Does the wind carry them

From some distant land

And plant them in my heart?

Do my dreams come

As twinkling stars

Falling from outer space?

Or are they intricately woven

Into my brain

Like a delicate piece of lace?

One moment they appear so clear.

The next instant, gone!

Like a flash of lightening

Within my mind,

The details don't linger long.

Some flicker like a lightening bug

Others are crystal clear.

I grasp them tightly

Holding fast

Lest they disappear.

So, I take my pencil in my hand

Writing pictures that I see.

On a sticky pad,

A napkin close,

Whatever space is free.

To my surprise, an image appears,

Painted by words alone.

How they come,

I do not know,

But I claim them as my own.

All of a sudden, I recognize

What these words really mean.

An open mind

Sprinkled with hope

Is one way of capturing a dream.

8 Be Still

Quiet early morning visits,

Peaceful moments with You Lord

Are treasured times free of cluttered thoughts.

The flavor of Your grace

Is sweetness to my faith.

You bring soothing comfort to my spirit.

You renew my soul.

In Your presence, I am free to be,

No more striving to prove my worth,

No more rushing to endless tasks.

Stillness flows like a gentle stream.

My heart opens like a flower at first bloom.

You welcome me to just relax,

To do nothing,

But enjoy Your amazing presence.

Like Mary, I am at the right place,

At Your feet Jesus, listening.

You show me what needs to be done,
Promising to be my light and way
As You guide me through my day.

Forgive me Lord when I rush past You,
Missing our morning quiet time.

How foolish I am, how sinful.
Keep my eyes focused on You, for in You
I find my purpose for living.
What more could I want or desire,
But to pour out Your love on others.

Thank You Lord for calling me
To be still and know that You are my Lord,
My Savior, who will carry me into eternity.

When You wrapped me in Your blood,
Forgiving me of all my sins and calling me Your
child,

Victory over death was Your gift of life to me.

I come in humble praise and thank You, O Lord.

Amen.

9 Boundless Enthusiasm

"The prompt for our next month's circle meeting is our passion," I told my friend as we sat at her kitchen table having tea. "It beats me what I'm going to write about."

"Why, Bette, you are passionate about a lot of things," she quickly responded.

"I am? Like what?" I asked wrinkling my brow.

"Well, you are always working in your yard and flower garden. I've watched you dig up the old wild grass in your front yard. Then get down on your hands and knees and sift the soil through your fingers pulling out all the roots. You nurture marigolds from seed. You take cuttings from other bushes and start new plants. You work hard creating your beautiful garden. That takes great energy."

"I don't think that calls for passion. I've played in the dirt all my life."

"Well, what about your writing? You spend hours working on a poem or a story. You redid your spare bedroom, organizing it into a writer's paradise. There are bookcases, filing cabinets, stacks of trays for writing projects. You have designed booklets full of your life stories for your family. And talk about books—you are always buying books to learn how to improve your skill. And how many people do you know that have a thirty by sixty-inch desk plus three printers?"

"I must admit I do spend a lot of time at my computer. It all started when my daughter-in-law bought me one of those fill-in-the-blank books. You know the kind where you tell your grandchildren what you were like when you were a kid, what your favorite color is, the songs you memorized, and on and on as if my life could be contained on one page. I mean, what kind of flower was it? What colorful blossoms appear in the spring? Were they wild or did I plant them and where? Too much information for the little spaces provided in that book. But passionate about writing, I don't know?" I pondered.

"What about your church work and your relationship with the Lord? Your life is lived by the teachings found in Scripture. You attend two Bible Studies a week and have daily devotions. You can't say that doesn't call for passion. And what about all the prayer groups you have started and the retreats you have led? Bette, open up your eyes. You are just an all-around passionate person."

"I am? But I love doing all those things, my friend. They aren't work. They don't take any special motivation. I just have a strong desire to do my best at whatever I'm doing. Maybe I don't understand the meaning of passion. I guess I need to go home and check the dictionary for its meaning. That's probably my problem. Hopefully then, I'll come up with something to write about."

10 The Finish Line

Please don't rush me, I know my pace.

You'll burn me out before the race.

Easy does it, I will perform.

I just go slower than the norm.

My brain it runs in circles fast.

The thoughts whiz by though seldom last.

A word or two will trigger more.

But too much pressure shuts the door.

If you will give more time to me.

The task at hand will finished be.

So easy does it, the race is won,

By catching the words, one by one.

11 Truckload of Grace

The light dimmed in my soul
As the forces of darkness
Pulled me deeper into depression.

Fighting to survive,
I jumped into my car
Heading to who knows where.

Stopping at a traffic light,
I noticed a large truck to my left.
The word grace was painted
In large letters on its side.

"Grace, it whispered to me, my grace!
It is sufficient for today's troubles.
Don't be so down cast, trust me."

Within seconds,
Like a light bulb displacing the darkness,

My depression dissolved and my soul was freed.

Hope replaced the misery eating away at me.

Laughter exploded releasing the tension

And filled my heart with joy, the Lord's joy.

At that moment,

I realized the writing on the truck

Had been planned long before time began.

For who, but God, would use a Grace Chemical truck

To save me from myself.

12 Celebrating Memories

The date is July fifth, 2012. I turned seventy-six today. I'm surprised how quickly the years have accumulated. A steaming cup of tea quiets my racing mind as I sit alone struggling to recall a lifetime of experiences. The telephone interrupts my memories about one of our most unforgettable Thanksgiving Days.

"Happy Birthday, Gramma," the voice says. "It's me, Shelby."

"Well, thank you, honey. So, what's happening in Texas these days?"

Forty-five minutes are filled with stories of starting college at the Art Institute of Houston, details of the fun she had vacationing in Colorado with her parents, and news about the young men in her life. They are only friends, she insists.

"Well, got to run, Gramma. I'll keep you updated on how college goes. I love you. Bye."

As I sit drinking in how precious our relationship is, my thoughts drift back to that special Thanksgiving Day when Shelby was only three.

Our home buzzed with excitement as thirteen members of our family came together. The table overflowed with tasty morsels surrounding the turkey. Once the meal was devoured, the men retreated to the living room to watch a football game. Some napped.

The women cleared the table, stored the leftover food, and began the monumental task of hand-washing the dishes. China and crystal always graced the table for holiday meals and never went into the dishwasher.

Loud explosions of laughter erupted as water splashed over the sink. Unforgettable conversations developed as the towels whipped the silverware dry and pans clattered as they found their way back into the cupboard. Cleanup after these large meals definitely was not for the faint of heart.

Normally, we would join the men, but not this year. I had planned a surprise project for the seven of us. I dragged out the hot glue guns, rolls of festive ribbon, a box of Christmas decorations, and a string of lights. Then I brought in a huge Christmas wreath and placed it on the table.

For two hours, excited chatter filled the room. We created large red bows, attaching them along with gold twine and large red and white velvet flowers. Christmas balls, holly berries, and the string of lights finished the project. With the wreath completed, we had the men hang it on the front of our house where it would announce the coming Christmas season and echo the joy of our fun together.

Revisiting these precious memories come as an unexpected birthday present from my family. Although they are totally unaware of their gift today, I am truly blessed by the joy they have given me throughout the many years of my life.

13 My Friends

All my life, I have been blessed with friends.
Some I have recognized,
While others have stood in the shadows.
Some I chose, while others have chosen me.
Some have come and gone,
And yet, a handful have remained.

They have influenced my life,
Teaching me how to love and laugh,
Opening my eyes to wonder
That was lost to my busyness.
They have generously offered forgiveness
When I have carelessly spoken.

My friends have helped me see myself
From a different point of view,
Often nudging me beyond my comfort zone.
Their listening ears have patiently received
Stories of joy and suffering,

And endless chatter with little meaning.

Our friendships have grown

As time has bound us together

Like a finely woven fabric.

So many hours spent shopping, sharing meals,

And volunteering in helping others,

No amount of money can touch their value.

Who could have dreamed the imprint

They would leave on my heart and soul,

As we walked through life together?

For each and every one of them,

I am truly grateful they touched my life,

And I am privileged to call them my friends.

14 The Teacher of God's Good News

There he sat

In front of the class

Eager to share The Good News.

A banquet he served

Of spiritual foods

Inviting all to come by

Like the apostle Paul

He gave it his all

Spending his life on The Good News.

So, a small number came

Who were never the same

Having eaten his spiritual pie.

In sickness and health

He shared his wealth

Risking to teach The Good News

His prayers were deep

And his studies complete

The Word he helped us apply.

Then one sad day

The Lord called him away

Our teacher of God's Good News.

We are richer indeed

Cause he was willing to lead

And our hunger he did satisfy.

This wise gentle man

Will live again

Because he believed The Good News

So, if you haven't heard

The truth in the Word

We urge you, come taste and know why

For it's our turn to teach

The message he preached

And we're eager to share The Good News.

All Scripture is God-breathed
and is useful for teaching, rebuking, correcting
and training in righteousness, so that the man of God
may be thoroughly equipped for every good work.
2 Timothy 3:16–17 NIV

In loving memory of Rev. Roger Robinson who was
the Teacher of God's GOOD NEWS

15 Remembering the Storms

It is August,

And summer has once again overstayed her

welcome.

Temperatures soar,

Reaching breathtaking highs in the mid-nineties.

Oh, for just an evening of cool breezes to sooth my

soul.

Yet, memories of the storms of two thousand four

Bring shivers to my body.

The deadly season started with Hurricane Charlie in

August,

Followed by Frances and then, Jeanne on September

twenty-fifth.

They brought six weeks of pure hell, death and

destruction.

As Jeanne raged on and on, heading our way,

My husband and I left our manufactured home

And found safety at a friend's residence.

The dark boiling clouds and pounding winds
Sent me scurrying under the covers of a bed.
I prayed for our protection.

The window panes quivered as the winds intensified.
Readings of seventy-nine to one hundred five miles
per hour
Were reported on the radio.

Trees fell like dominoes
Littering yards with debris.
Once the storm passed,
Caravans of trucks
Hauled away their skeletons.
Scared landscapes stood as monuments
To the powerful hurricane.

News reports told of boats being swallowed up
By the swirling waters,
While beachfront properties lost their pools

To the ocean.

Winds of one hundred twenty miles per hour

Terrified residents of Florida for one full minute

That seemed an eternity.

She caused over seven billion dollars' worth of

damage.

History often repeats itself.

Therefore, I am praying for a quiet August this year.

So much for wanting a cool breeze,

Just let the storms pass us by this fall, if You will.

And keep us thankful for Your hand of protection,

Lord.

16 Free at Last

I wonder what is going on.

Every day brings so many changes, so many new

developments

My quarters are getting really cramped and I can't

speak up.

Where are the people who are supposed to enforce

children's rights?

I want more protection.

I'm carried around like a bag of potatoes and no one

seems concerned.

My days have run into weeks, into months, yet time

seems to stand still.

Oops! Here we go again.

Mom and Dad, my sisters and I pile into our car.

Talk about overcrowding.

I wonder where we are going?

No one tells me anything.

Well, that didn't take long. We must have arrived.

Everyone is piling out of the car, dragging me along.

Finally, it is quiet again and I can rest.

Boy, was I mistaken.

Pow! Bang! Boom!

It sounds like gunshots, but everyone is applauding.

Ooh! Ahh! Ooo! How beautiful!

Let me see!

No fair, I can't see what's happening?

I can't make out the colors, but according to my

family's comments,

The shades must be awesome.

Pow! Bang! Boom! The noise continues.

Will someone please cover my ears?

I guess it's over as it is quiet again and we're piling

back into the car.

Packed in like sardines, and headed for the barn, my

Dad says.

I wonder what that means.

The night can't come soon enough. I'm tired.

I barely get to sleep and then, everyone is up again,

I wonder what all the commotion is about?

What the heck, who pulled the plug?

All the water is rushing down the drain pulling me
with it.

How am I supposed to escape through that little
hole?

Ouch! Talk about a tight fit!

Whoosh! What a wild ride.

I wonder where am I?

Hey, what's with the slap on the bottom?

Did I do something wrong?

There are those silly church bells ringing again,
always waking me up.

You know what I say to that?

Waaaaaahhh!

And so, I was born that Sunday at 7:30 a.m. as those
church bells chimed.

17 A Handkerchief

Long before the tissue came
each little girl did know,
a handkerchief in her pocket
was a must with furbelow.

Do you have a handkerchief,
a nice linen one will do,
with fancy lace surrounding it
and your initial on it too?

Perhaps yours is made of cotton
like the ones I had long ago,
the ones my mother used to tie
my nickel in for the picture show.

Tissues come and tissues go
but handkerchiefs come to stay,
like friends you keep them near your heart
and never throw them away.

18 A Welcomed Interruption

If I am very still,
I can hear it coming
far off in the distance.

Its carefully controlled bursts of fire
signals to me to look
beyond my task at hand.

As it passes over the roof tops
and through the silent wind,
I sense that even the dogs have joined in song,
as if to greet this slow-moving carriage.

Unlike the steel-coated train
which gets in my way,
This rainbow-colored giant floating lazily overhead
is a welcomed interruption.

For a few moments I am free,

free of the things that clutter my space;

free of the problems that I must face;

free to let my imagination drift;

to wonder what it's like to set upon the sky.

But like a dream,

when I open my eyes, it is gone.

How quickly I am caught up once again

in my hectic schedule; how sad,

for it strictly controls the course of my day.

19 Riding a Rainbow

For a sleepyhead like me, 6:00 a.m. rolled around much too soon on that dark June morning in 1986. The alarm blared, and the lights that hung above our bed flashed on declaring it was time to get up. There would be no grace period today for my mind to catch up with my husband's. He had made plans to meet our friends in Nokomis, Florida, at 8:30 a.m., for a day of fishing on the Gulf of Mexico. I wasn't very enthusiastic about the trip, but I dragged myself out of bed and stumbled blindly into the shower.

Once breakfast had found its way into my stomach, we headed out the door. It was exactly 7:00 a.m. when we backed out of the driveway. My husband, Russ, is a stickler about being on time, so after a few minutes into our excursion, it puzzled me when he pulled off into the Kmart parking lot.

"What are you doing?" I grumbled.

"Never you mind," he said. "I just want to check out that suspicious looking vehicle parked over there."

His FBI training kept him always scanning for such scenarios no matter where we went, so his unexplainable actions never surprised me anymore. He pulled into a parking slot and turned off the engine.

"Look over there. See that sheriff's car? Something is going on here I want to just watch for a minute."

I have learned over the years not to challenge him when he seems determined to do something, so I leaned back, closed my eyes, and rested.

"Oh, oh!" he said.

I quickly sat up, focusing my eyes, just in time to see a blue van headed in our direction. It stopped directly in front of our car.

"What's going on?" I questioned. "Why's that lady parking in front of us with all the other empty slots available to her? I wonder what her problem is?"

As she climbed out and headed toward our car, I noticed a sign on her van window stating: "Hot Air Balloon Rides."

"Surprise honey!" My husband laughed. "Happy fiftieth birthday."

"Oh dear! Are we really going for a hot air balloon ride?" I questioned. "But what about our fishing trip?"

"All a ruse to get you out of bed and on the road."

He climbed out of our car, still laughing, and spoke to the young woman for a few minutes. She instructed us to follow her to the empty lot at Highway Sixty and Valrico Road where her ground crew was already busily assembling the balloon we would soon be riding.

Ten minutes later, I stood in awe as her crew laid out yards of brightly colored nylon canvas. Strips of watermelon red, sky blue, taffy yellow, and more made up the huge structure that glistened in the early morning sun. The crew's professionalism left no doubt they were veterans at doing their jobs. Large fans blew air into the billowing chambers of the balloon until it gracefully began to lift off the ground. Once they attached the wicker basket, and the burner with its heavy tanks of propane, we were invited to climb aboard.

I was a little apprehensive, but our pilot reassured me that she hadn't lost a passenger yet. Russ helped me into the basket, and the three of us began our experience of a lifetime.

Slowly we rose into the heavens leaving behind all my anxiety. We seemed to float on the early morning dew. Silence was the music of the moment. Except for a periodic rush of air caused by the burst of orange flames needed to keep the sleeve inflated, the joy that enveloped me went uninterrupted. Childhood memories of merry-go-round rides flashed in my mind, but this time I wasn't on a horse.

I was riding a rainbow.

As we leisurely floated over our sprawling community, we took pictures of rooftops where friends lived. Dogs barked as we dipped toward the earth only to lift up again reaching greater heights. I felt like Mary Poppins, Peter Pan, and a fairy princess, all rolled up into one, as I tried to comprehend the unbelievable delight that stirred inside of me.

All too soon, the final descent lay before us. The time had flown by so quickly. In less than an hour, my view of my community had completely changed.

Then, ever so carefully, our pilot threaded the large balloon in between the high power lines that dotted Interstate 75.

"Brace yourselves!" she yelled. "We're about to land."

Thump! Thump! The basket bounced a couple of times, and then the ride was over. To our surprise, as we emerged from the safety of our nest, the pilot had us kneel down on the ground.

"It's a required tradition for all adventurers," she told us as she pulled out a book from her pocket.

She read a blessing of thanksgiving for our safe return to earth and proceeded to pour champagne over our heads.

"It's all part of the tradition," she repeated.

"What a waste of good champagne," I lamented.

As a final farewell, she drove us into Brandon and treated us to breakfast and laughter as we recalled the breathtaking events of the morning.

"Thank You" seemed so inadequate in comparison to the joy that I felt in my heart. This once in a lifetime birthday gift was, definitely, worth the loss of a few hours of sleep and one I will long remember.

20 Do It Now

Rise up, O Christians, from your sleep.

Brush off the sand from heads buried deep.

The time is now for action — take

A stand on issues, the difference — make.

Write letters to encourage those

Who work to serve with spirits bold.

And words of caution justly raised

Are deemed as vital as the praise.

Awake the nation to God's free grace.

His loving plan, our sins erase.

Without His help, our nation will fall.

And judgment untempered can crush us all.

So, rise up, O Christians, lend a hand.

For the time has come to cleanse our land.

21 Childhood Memories

Bits and pieces
 Of memories past,
Must catch them now
For they'll never last.

Beginning childhood
 So long ago,
All the fun times
Simply go.

The playhouse, dolls,
The hours spent
Enjoying the moments
They came and went.

The hop scotch, jacks
And a pick-up stick,
Nothing high tech
But they did the trick.

59

The joy of childhood
A glimpse in time,
Penny cancy
Bags for a cime.

    Had I kept a journal
    Way back then,
     And written it all down
    With a pencil or pen.

I wouldn't be here
 Struggling so,
To recapture the stories
From their whispering echo.

    But as I look back now
    And remember them,
    These flashbacks bring joy
    So, I'll commence again.

22 Rewards of Retirement

It's great getting older,
casting off tight shoes,
scratching where it itches,
serving where I choose.

It's great having leisure,
seeking fun that's free,
for my income is limited
so, it's fishing for me.

It's great sharing skills
I've learned all my life
with new friends I've found
including my wife.

It's great doing nothing,
but reading a book,
or taking a walk
along a cool brook.

It's great being older

with more time to pray

to discover the reason

I'm still here today.

There is a time for everything, and a season for

every activity under heaven.

Ecclesiastes 3:1 NIV

23 Christmas

It all began many years ago
As a very private thing.
There was Mary, Joseph, and an infant Son
Who was destined to be a king.

The weather was brisk; the night was dark;
There was a brilliant star above.
This little child, asleep in the straw,
Had come to teach of God's love.

The shepherds left their flocks that night,
To Bethlehem they came.
They sought this child, called "King of Jews,"
The wise men said the same.

The time has come to celebrate
This holy Christ child's birth.
The Son of God, our heavenly friend,
Brings peace to all on earth.

24 More Than a Christmas Tree

Several years ago, my family and I went searching for the perfect Christmas tree. We looked several places and finally found one tree that came close. It was tall with a sturdy trunk. The needles were firm and when crushed between our fingers released a pine scent that was heavenly.

It had one slight flaw. Several branches were missing from one side. The salesperson suggested that if that section were placed against the wall, no one would notice, so we bought it. When the tree was fully decorated, it was beautiful.

The Christmas season quickly sped by. We returned all the trimmings to their boxes and put them in the attic. Our once beautiful tree lay waiting for the trash pickup.

A friend suggested we keep the trunk for Lent. "Cut off the top and create a cross," she said. "It makes a great

Easter statement." The idea was intriguing, so we kept tree.

When Lent arrived, we trimmed off the branches, cut the trunk into two pieces, and bound them together with a cord. The front flowerbed was chosen to hold our makeshift cross. From there, all who passed by could easily see it.

Once the cross was in place, we hung a crown on it; a crown made from cuttings I had persuaded a local nurseryman to give me. They came from a cactus that had sharp, dried spikes protruding from its branches. It was all but dead, making it a perfect choice for a crown. But not until the man told us the name of the cactus was the Crown of Thorns did we realize just how perfect it was. It would hang from the cross all through the Lenten season carrying its unspoken message.

We received many comments. Some were encouraging: "What a clever use of your Christmas tree" and "How perfect, the trunk is like a bridge connecting Christmas to Easter." Others were less kind. Some even suggested we were bordering on being fanatical about our faith. "You better be careful. What will people think?" But the cross stayed.

Holy week arrived. It had been almost forty days since the dried branches were formed into a circle and placed on the cross. Much to our amazement, little green leaves began to appear. Life had remained where we had seen none. I explained to my children that a cactus can live for a long time without nourishment, but I couldn't explain why the plant chose to set leaves during Holy week.

We draped the cross with a purple cloth on Maundy Thursday and with a black one on Good Friday. Early Easter morning we placed a white satin drape on the crossbar. We added plastic Easter lilies and a sign that read, "He is risen."

As I was about to remove the crown of thorns, we discovered three red flowers had bloomed overnight.

Tears streamed down my face. How the plant chose to bloom on Easter morning remained a mystery I could not explain. We agreed the crown must stay for others to see how God's creativity far out-surpassed ours.

On Monday, we took the cross down and threw it away. I cut the dried branches that had formed the crown into several pieces and planted them in the flowerbed. Before long, several of the stems returned to their original state. They were bright green and full of life. Eventually more of the delicate red blossoms appeared. It was an awesome sight.

The years have brought many changes into the lives of my children and me, but time has not been able to remove the memory of this event. I am so thankful I did not succumb to the ridicule. What a tragedy it would have been to have missed God's gift of this special Christmas tree and its crown.

25 To His Glory

Thoughts

silent thoughts

roam the chambers of my mind

linking together into untold stories

until at last they seek to be freed

by the keys which will give them life

while God gives them meaning and purpose

for it was to His glory

that they were first

conceived.

26 Dreams

Now, I'm not talking about
The dreams that appear
Out of nowhere
While I'm fast asleep.

I'm speaking of the ones
That give my life meaning,
That propel me forward
Into unknown territory.

These dreams are the fuel
That drives my creativity.
They push me to try new things,
To discover joy beyond the limits
I often set for myself.

Dreams seem to open doors
Locked by my fear of failure.
They stimulate my soul

And give me hope
Where belief once lay fragile and weak.

These strange but wonderful thoughts
Take me to magical places.
They frequently hold answers
To questions I have yet to ask.

My dreams give me the ability
To see myself as others see me.
They give me the courage
To follow new paths.

Oh, beautiful, wonderful, precious dreams,
Carry me onward to the place
Where love fills the spirit
And words flow like the river of life.

Let me soar as the eagles fly
Or be content to ride on butterfly wings.
Whatever your mission,
Dear dreams of mine,

I'm ready to follow, just lead the way.

27 Carolina Song Birds

Do you know what a messenger of God looks like?
Do they have the seal of the Lord stamped on their
forehead?
Do they come carrying the cross and Holy Scriptures?
I believe not.

My image of a messenger looks just like you, like me.
Take the ones my Carolina friend sings with.
Twice a week they travel up to thirty-five miles to
sing to patients locked away in nursing homes
bringing the love of God to those often-forgotten souls.

They sit like zombies amazed that these song birds
come to give dignity to them, many of whom are
dying. The music helps them drift back in time
recalling happier days when their lives
were once vibrant and strong.

Many

cared for others,

some now with crippled hands

recall how their fingers flowed over the ivory keys at

concert halls or sculptured award-winning statues.

Like magic, the melodies wrap these patients in the

grace of God bringing joy to their sagging spirits

if only for a few moments.

Their weakened bodies, their dissolving bones

are forgotten while the music speaks to them.

The notes play in their tired minds while the

sweetness brings a healing balm,

an aromatic fragrance to their

hearts.

Bless these song birds who

give of themselves to lift others.

May these messengers realize they are standing

on holy ground of those soon to meet our Lord.

So, sing on song birds, you have been called by our

Father to do this special work.

May your voices delight these precious children
of God and offer up praise to His glory.

28 Deadly Beauty

I was seven, maybe eight
When winter hurled a deadly ice storm
Into my neighborhood.

At first glance, everything appeared as a fairyland.
Stalactites of icy crystals sparkled in the morning
light.
They hung precariously from the rooftops, windows
sills and flower boxes.
Spider web art graced the windowpanes.
The landscape was breathtaking,
Yet, strangely eerie.

Trees encased in frozen dress bent low.
Branches, strained from the load,
Sent limbs crashing to the ground.
Telephone lines stretched beyond their limits,
Snapped,
And whipped violently in the wind.

Early spring flowers woke to blankets of the bitter chill.

Spikes of frozen grass crunched under our feet.

Everything was encased in the frigid ice droplets,

Shimmering like diamonds in the blinding light.

The creativity proved magnificent.

Then, its beauty was quickly overshadowed

As the temperatures rose,

Allowing hours of powdery flakes to be added to the

landscape.

Blustery winds whipped the snow into towering

drifts

Forming treacherous highways concealing patches of

black ice

Waiting for an unsuspecting motorist to spin out of

control.

Hazardous, terrifying, spine-chilling were words

tossed about

by those daring to venture out.

The deadly fairyland lasted for three days,

Leaving behind

A collection of crumpled vehicles,

Damaged lives,

And countless victims

Whose days were frozen in time.

29 Laughter and Lace

When you were a child, what games did you love playing?

Back in the late thirties and forties, before computers, we played board games, card games, marbles, jacks, tag, and all sorts of games using balls. My favorite pastime involved old lace curtains, discarded sheets, and blankets whose soft colorful ribbon trim had seen its better days. A few of mother's old dresses and a pair of high-heeled shoes added to the fun. All one needed was an immense imagination, and the magic lasted for hours. We called it Dress-Up Time.

Trips to the Toledo Art Museum fueled our creativity. In the basement of this magnificent building were models of kings and queens, first ladies, emperors, and famous movie stars—all elaborately displayed inside glass cases. They stood about two feet tall. Crafted out of wax, these dolls wore outfits made of silks, satins, and velvets trimmed with pearls and gemstones. A variety of furs added to their elegance. I would stand glued in place until my sisters dragged me away.

With hard times lasting year after year, money wasn't available to buy anything comparable to these gorgeous fashions. But my mother did her best to sew many adorable outfits for my sisters and me.

In high school, I elected to take a sewing class. I started with a white cotton slip, received a B. Then I made a purple wool skirt with a crooked seam. The instructor gave me a D. I advanced to designing aprons, blouses, more skirts, slacks, and eventually dresses, ending up with an A for the class.

When I lived in Abilene, Texas, and money was scarce again, I sewed outfits for my neighbor. The extra money helped put food on the table.

When my son came along, I learned the art of installing zippers in his trousers. Then came suit jackets and velvet vests. Four years later, my daughter was born. Little girl outfits were a joy to make, as were her doll clothes. Using yellow dotted Swiss material, I took her bunk bed and transformed it into a delightful canopy bed, ruffles and all. I covered her rocking chair with the same material, and even made her doll a dress.

I sewed miniskirts I wore as a Boy Scout Den Mother and purple bell-bottoms as a Youth Ministry leader in my church. I wrote skits for the women in my church, especially for district conventions that required designing and sewing costumes. From fairy tale characters to circus performers, the fun never stopped.

As material and patterns became more expensive than what I could buy outfits for on sale, my sewing machine went idle. It came out of its case only to hem a skirt or mend a torn sleeve.

When I married Russell in October 1978, I discovered he was involved in numerous organizations. Because of his leadership position, we attended many fancy functions, requiring upscale outfits. So, Cinderella left her kitchen job and went shopping. There were classy black suits and dressy dresses, a mink fur and beaded purses—it was, once again, time for Dress-Up!

For almost thirty-three years my closet was filled with satin and lace gowns, long white gloves, and glamorous eveningwear. My favorite gown is one my sister Bobbi gave me. It is made of gold silk fabric purchased in Japan. It has a large matching shawl. It is so beautiful, I can't part with it.

Since Russell's death in 2010, many of my gowns have been sold through consignment shops. But a few still linger in my back closet waiting their turn to be recycled as Halloween costumes. Playing Cinderella has never lost its luster, and I hope the laughter continues forever.

30 The Giver of Wisdom

In the midst of the hustle, bustle
Of your daily life,
With all the noise and chatter,
With all its pressing demands that matter,
I urge you to come, sit a spell with me
And I will take you to places
Far beyond your understanding.

I will carry you like a magic carpet
Into the silent realm of words
With all their beauty, wonder, and wisdom.
I will be your friend, your teacher,
And share with you the priceless gift
Only you can claim.

But beware, mine is not the only manuscript.
There are countless volumes
Waiting to draw you into their world.
Evil often hides within their pristine pages

Waiting to lead you astray.

So choose wisely, my child, who you allow

To shape your thinking.

Question the logic, the validity, the intent

Of their works,

For they hold the power to change your life forever.

Protect your heart, your mind, your spirit.

When satisfied the words mean you no harm,

Drink deeply from their fountains of truth

Until you become filled with the wisdom

Of the Giver.

The beginning of wisdom is this: Get wisdom.

Though it cost all you have, get understanding.

Proverbs 4:7 NIV

31 Listen

In the early morning silence,

the fan blades gently whisper,

"It's time to wake up.

Don't miss the first music of the day.

The songbirds have gathered

rehearsing their melodies.

Come sit on the porch,

watch the world come alive

as the sun parts the darkness."

Off in the distance

the hum of the tires

of the early morning risers

adds to the harmony.

Then, the harsh shrill of an oncoming train,

the squealing brakes of a semi truck

and the choir of irresponsible barking dogs

destroys the magic of the moment

overriding the breathtaking concerto

lost to another day.

32 Christmas Cookies

Our family tradition of baking Christmas cookies started with my grandmother Lena Schaefer. She loved to bake cakes and pies, but her lard-based sugar cookies were her specialty. When my family visited Grandmother, her cookie jar was always full, just waiting for us, especially at Christmas.

Once when my sister, Carole, and I spent the week with Grandmother, we got to watch as she created her famous sugar cookies. Flour floated in the air as she dumped the ingredients together. Holding the bowl tightly against her apron, she stirred the mixture until it reached just the right consistency.

Next, she formed the creamy white dough into round circles large enough to cover a saucer. No little cookies for Grandmother. After sticking an extra-large raisin right in the center of each cookie, she'd pop them in the oven. The aroma of sweet dough baking filled the house. I can remember sitting at her kitchen table with a large glass of cold milk, eating them while they were still warm.

Grandmother passed her love for baking down to my mother who learned to bake bread from scratch. She could make the flakiest pie crusts that would melt in your mouth, then fill them with bright red cherries or tart apple slices, lemon or chocolate pudding. Cakes and cookies took less effort except when she allowed us little girls to join in the fun at Christmas.

When I got married and had children, the making of Christmas cookies began the week after Thanksgiving. Both my son and daughter donned aprons and joined me in the preparation. Measuring cups, rolling pins, cutting boards, cookie sheets, and cooling racks would quickly cover the kitchen counter tops.

Shakers of colored sugar and candy drops were dug out from the back of the cupboard. White sugar, flour, baking soda, and baking powder; vanilla, milk, and butter; mixing bowls and measuring spoons—all were retrieved from the pantry and the refrigerator. The clanging of pots and pans joined the excitement as the favorite recipes were carefully chosen from my dog-eared Betty Crocker cookbook.

Sugar cookies were a given, but mine never quite tasted like Grandmother's. Then date nut bars dusted in confectioners' sugar would be next. Oatmeal, peanut butter, and snickerdoodle cookies often made the list. Springerle bars took much longer and were made long after the children were in bed.

The rolling of dough for sugar cookies, to the dusting of flour on the floor, were all part of the labor of love shared. Choosing the right cookie cutter took great concentration and sometimes, produced enormous results. Laughter filled the kitchen as individual creations were placed on the cookies sheets readied for the oven. I don't know who had the most fun, my children or myself. Call me sentimental, but I still have the tin filled with the original cutters. I can't seem to part with them.

I am blessed with a loving daughter-in-law, Christine, who has allowed me to pass this tradition on to her and her daughter. Each year we go through the same routine of picking the recipes, buying the ingredients, and setting up a day to bake. One year at her home and the next in my kitchen. I call it, *"sharing the joy and mess."*

Up until the year my mother died at ninety-three, she would join us in our baking extravaganzas. Four generations of cooks in the same kitchen turned out some very special memories. Shelby, my granddaughter, turned fifteen her last birthday, and I'm thrilled she plans on continuing our family tradition of sharing time together in the baking of Christmas cookies.

33 Sunday Morning

Off in the distance
a dove welcomed the morning.
A screeching gull competed
with the sound of the rolling surf.
The slap of the beach runner's feet
added to the melody.

The early morning risers
curiously scrutinized the water's edge
for the best treasures the sea had to offer.
Avid walkers gazed at their hand-held toys
missing the majestic seascape spread out before them.
Fishing boats appeared on the horizon.

A gentle breeze carried the aroma of salt water
as storm clouds slowly moved in our direction.
In minutes, angry gray clouds developed
forcing the small fishing boats to hover near shore.

A dazzling bolt of lightning exploded from the
heavens
as icy droplets of rain pelted all who dared remain.

The Lord claimed Sunday morning as His own.
Protected by my porch, I was blessed to experience
His powerful voice and stunning beauty no one can
defy.

34 Answer Please

"Who do they say I am," asked Jesus?

"Who do they say I am?"

The son of Mary, a trouble maker,

And some say you're a sham.

"Who do they say I am," quizzed Jesus?

"Who do they say I be?"

A storyteller, the Baptist's friend

Who made the blind man see.

"Who do they say I am," asked Jesus?

"Who do they say I am?"

God's own Son, who came to earth,

To be our Passover lamb.

"Who do they say I am," quizzed Jesus?

"Who do they say I be?"

There is no doubt, our Savior King,

Our way to eternity.

"And who do you say I am," asked Jesus?

"Who do you say I am?"

"Who do you say I am," quizzed Jesus?

"Who do you say I be?"

The next day

John saw Jesus coming toward him

and said, "Look, the Lamb of God,

who takes away the sin of the

world."

John 1:29 NIV

35 Mother's Garden

To some people the return of spring means the beginning of warmer weather and time to enjoy the outdoors. Baseball, riding bikes, planting flowers, taking hikes, and picnics would all make their lists. As for me, I looked forward to school being almost over. But that isn't what my mother had on her mind. No sir! Spring meant one thing to her . . . preparing the soil for her vegetable garden.

Weeds, growing in the rich black dirt that once was a field for cows and horses, grew as tall as me and had to be pulled out. Their roots were deep and strong having begun their evil task the previous fall.

Turning the earth and raking out the unwanted plants left my small hands aching. The work was hard, but Mother saw it as a labor of love. She seemed to forget everything else that had to be done when she gardened.

The plot of soil lay in our backyard, and I guess it covered an area about twelve feet by twenty-four feet. No small task, mind you, for this twelve-year old boy. Beads of sweat rolled down my face and after spending several days *playing in the dirt,* as my Mother called it, my back throbbed like a bad tooth. By the time all the weeds were gone, I found a reason to be gone as well. She didn't seem to mind.

She spent days measuring the rows, mounding the soil, and carefully dropping the seeds in one at a time. There were packages of lettuce seeds, carrot seeds, onion sets, cherry tomato sets, small pepper plants—all lovingly and carefully placed in the bed ready for their response to her tender care.

I never quite understood her relentless drive to create the vegetable garden. I remember Grandmother had a garden. Maybe that is where Mom learned to love working the soil.

It wasn't all bad. We ate salads fresh from the garden until the summer heat beat the plants down. I loved pulling up the carrots and radishes when they were ready to harvest. We could just pop the cherry tomatoes in our mouths whenever visiting the backyard. Gardening did have its rewards.

The year we planted potatoes was the best. I had no idea what to expect, but Mother did. Dark green bush like plants pushed up through the mounds of dirt. Weeks later, we turned over the soil and what once were small pieces of raw potatoes had produced a pile of babies. Actually, they were quite large. My younger sister and I just wiped off the dirt and ate them raw.

Then there was the year we planted corn. The stalks grew tall, and Mother took extra care tending to their needs. Unfortunately, the cornstalk borers took their toll on the ears that formed, and, because Mother didn't believe in using chemicals, there was little to show for all her hard work. I felt bad for her, but what did survive tasted sweet.

Bugs and diseases flourish here in Florida because we have only a few cold days of winter. Things like spider mites, aphids, grubs, and armyworms never stopped Mother. Every spring she would begin again.

When I graduated from high school, my parents divorced. Mother sold the house, and I joined the Army. Eventually she remarried, and my sister went to live with my dad.

I don't think Mother ever worked another garden after that, and I have often wondered if that made her sad.

36 Miracle Moments

In my early fifties, the Lord led me to create a Gospel Clown ministry. The idea both surprised and astounded me as I never saw myself as a clown. The idea angered my husband who couldn't understand why I would do such a foolish thing.

"What would people think?" he growled, as his Marine mentality emerged.

But the Spirit moved me forward, undaunted by his threats, and doors opened before I even knew where I was going. For three and a half years, I put on the grease paint of the white-faced clown and entertained children of all ages in my striped suit, curly hair, and pockets filled with hand puppets.

There were visits to our local hospital and birthday parties to attend. Marching in our community's Fourth of July Parade and invitations to charity events were scheduled.

I developed Workshops for Women led by my Crazy Lady Clown donned in her curly rainbow hair and matching candy-striped stockings. A long green feather boa complimented her colorful short dress, revealing ruffled white bloomers gathered with red ribbons.

Then several circumstances forced me to stop, from the unrelenting pressure from my husband to a breast cancer scare. I cleaned and packed away all my costumes. Tears filled my eyes. I felt that season of my life was over, until a teacher from a local public elementary school called me.

"I work with seven autistic students," he began. "I'm developing a grant to have a mime come and interact with them. They range from eight to twelve years of age. Research has proven that autistic students often relate to a mime."

"My wife and I have been praying for someone and your name has been given to us," he continued. "Would you be willing to come to the school for forty-five minutes each Friday for the next eighteen weeks? Actually, you would only have to stay for ten to fifteen minutes at best. Their attention span is extremely limited."

"I don't know," I said hesitantly. "I've all but given up my clown ministry."

"Oh please, pray about it as it would mean so much to me and my students," he said.

"I'll speak to my husband, but I can't promise anything."

I said goodbye and hung up the phone.

"Who was that?" my husband asked.

Reluctantly, I explained what the teacher had said. The frown on my husband's face told me before he even said anything he was totally against the idea.

"You don't even know how to be a mime," he snapped. "This conversation is over."

Six weeks later, the teacher called again.

"My grant has come through, and I'm now able to pay you thirty-five dollars for each day you come to class," he said, as his voice reached a high pitch. "Perhaps this will change your husband's mind."

Once again, I spoke to my husband who half-heartedly approved of the idea when he found out I would be paid. He still couldn't believe someone would offer me money just to be silly, but silly wasn't what God had in mind.

The following week, I met with the teacher, observed the students, went through the details, signed a contract, and set up a schedule. Now the real work began. I prayed to the Lord seeking guidance. I felt totally unprepared when Friday rolled around.

I slipped into my black leotards, stockings, and black tennis shoes. I pulled on a long-sleeve white knit turtleneck shirt adding white gloves and topped it off with a multicolored straw bowler hat. Taking a deep breath, I hopped into my car, and headed to the school.

From the very beginning the students were completely intrigued with my mime. The ten to fifteen minutes the teacher suggested turned into forty-five minutes. Finally, he stopped me, so he could continue his schedule.

"I can hardly believe how the students stayed focused," he exclaimed. "Thank you so much. I can't wait for next week's session."

"Me either," I thought.

I worked up a routine using an imaginary broom and dustpan to start our time together. I swept some dirt into a make-believe dustpan and dumped it into an imaginary wastebasket. I opened my suitcase and removed a pretend rug and placed it in front of me. Then I sat down and read a make-believe book, turning the pages and silently laughing.

One of the students, a precious young boy about eight, with sandy brown hair, sad brown eyes, with an average build and neatly dressed every day, always sat next to my right. He never spoke, but his eyes, filled with intense concentration, followed my every move. After three Fridays, the repetitive playacting developed an unexpected consequence.

The next week when I opened my suitcase filled with all my props, he stepped forward and took out the imaginary broom, dustpan, rug, and book. He proceeded to mimic my entire skit. Once the rug lay on the floor, he motioned for me to sit down, and we read the pretend book together.

I was dumbstruck. Somehow my routine had penetrated the fog and pierced the unseen barrier autism creates. The teacher told me later the boy's mother was ecstatic.

The following week, I brought a real child's broom, dustpan, small throw rug, and a large colorful picture book. He beamed as he went through the entire skit. As we sat on the rug together, I can't explain the energy, the excitement, and the sense of accomplishment that radiated from this young boy's face. I was humbled beyond words.

Recalling this incident still gives me goose bumps and this was only one of many magical moments I was privileged to experience while interacting with these unique autistic students.

Call it silliness, foolishness, or whatever you will, I saw God's love working through my mime reaching these young people who are tragically imprisoned in a world known only to them.

37 The Artist

I've painted the town
a few times in my life,
and puttered in oil
with canvas and knife,
but it pleased me the most
when I exchanged my frown,
for a bright happy smile
using the oils of the clown.

I purchased some curls
to surround my mask,
and made me a suit
just right for the task.
I added white gloves
and shoes that were old,
some wild colored stockings
with stripes so bold.

I filled both my pockets

with hand puppets and more,

a noisy red horn

and balloons galore.

Yet, I wasn't complete

till God filled my heart,

with His love and His purpose

for mastering this art.

For we are God's handiwork; created in Christ Jesus

to do good works, which God prepared in advance

for us to do.

Ephesians 2:10 NIV

38 A Box of Socks

In my dresser drawer
There is a box.
And in the box
Are oodles of socks
All neatly standing in full view.

In the box,
In my dresser drawer
That is filled with oodles of socks,
Are red socks, green ones, some are blue,
Yellow socks, pink ones and white ones too.
Some are old and some are new.

In the box of colored socks,
In my dresser drawer,
Are butterflies and snowmen,
Lady bugs and giraffes
And one pair has stripes;

Red, white and blue.

They all remind me of a crazy zoo.

In the box of bright colored socks

In my dresser drawer

Are happy socks and dancing socks,

Socks for walking and bedtime, too.

There are just so many silly socks,

Won't you come try on a pair or two?

39 The Call

"Hello."

I sense joy

Bubbling from a happy heart

when you answer.

Expressions of bliss

Tumble from your lips.

The tone

Is like a spinning kaleidoscope

of color.

It resonates like a child's

upon discovering the presents

Under the Christmas tree.

Yet, your voice,

Soft as baby skin,

Whispers in my ears.

Your outlook,

Like a wandering brook,

Charms my heart as you glide

From thought to thought.

The call ends much too soon

With a cheerful, "Good bye."

40 A Welcomed Change

Spring arrives in late April in South Dakota. Unfortunately, we headed to Rapid City in early February in 1960 where thirty-two degrees was the norm. One would wonder how winter could ever give up her hold on the freezing temperatures that keep the earth her prisoner.

The temperature in Bradenton, Florida, when we left that February and headed north, was seventy-two degrees. We had little advance notice of what lay ahead. Home computers were a thing of the future. Hourly weather reports on television were still in the works.

As each mile clicked away, tiny piles of snow began to slowly appear along the roadsides. They were a foreshadow of things to come.

My husband, Don, our two-month-old son, David, and myself, watched in amazement as the mounds of white frozen crystals steadily rose along the edge of the road. The afternoon sun danced on the snowdrifts, creating a fantasy of sparkling diamond shrouds. The sight was both exhilarating and scary.

The warm breezes of Florida steadily gave way to chillier temperatures as we drove north. When we stopped for gasoline and lunch in South Dakota, we watched in amazement, as our breath became frost right before our eyes.

Don's new assignment with the Air Force had been the reason for our winter adventure. After serving a year in Baffin Island near Greenland, he had asked for a southern base. We saw this assignment as a bad joke.

The narrow road through this northern tundra, as we viewed it, was lined with snowdrifts, unlike anything we had ever experienced.

"They appear like giant white walls," I exclaimed.

As we moved through the state, these walls eventually gave way to snowdrifts controlled by what we later learned were called snow fences. We both grew up in northern Ohio, but we were not prepared for the long, drawn-out winters that lay ahead of us.

Once we settled into our little home away from home, winter did her best to discourage us with temperatures as low as forty-two degrees below zero. I felt like a bear hibernating in our modest apartment, seldom venturing out except to hang diapers on the clothesline, go to the base for groceries, or go to church.

David often wore his snowsuit to bed to keep warm.

Huddled together in our rented apartment, we waited for the spring thaw. It was a long time coming, and was a welcomed change worth celebrating.

We spent two and a half years stationed at Ellsworth Air Force Base, enduring a climate filled with surprises.

Besides the snow, spring rains brought flooding, and golf ball sized hail slammed against the house during summer storms making large dents in the siding and destroying all my rose bushes I had planted in the front yard. Without a carport or garage, our new car also took a severe beating. To make things worse, summer lasted only two and a half months, and fall slipped quickly into winter.

I have great respect for the people who live in South Dakota, but returning to the South could not come soon enough. I thanked the Lord that we had survived when Don's time for us to move on arrived. New orders sent us to the barren country next to the desert where a radar site was located. Eagle Pass, Texas, was as hot and dry as Rapid City, South Dakota, was cold and wet.

Eventually Don mustered out of the Air Force, and we headed back to Florida. Spring in Bradenton welcomed us with warm weather, trees covered with purple, red, and pink blossoms. Everywhere lush green foliage greeted us.

If I never see another snowflake again, I'm good.

41 The Promised Place

The sun rose and poured forth her warmth on me.

And I woke from what seemed to have been a long

deep sleep.

But the brightness sent me scurrying into the

shadows.

For the beauty it revealed was too magnificent.

A strange force seemed to beckon me to return.

Even though my body trembled with fear,

Fear of the unknown.

Fear of the possibility that I did not belong in this

place,

I crept closer to the light.

A sense of welcome enveloped me.

I could tell that this was a place created for kings and

queens

Its elegance far surpassed anything I could imagine.

Everything glowed with life, and so did I.

I felt like I was seeing and hearing for the first time,

Feeling love and loved for the first time.

There was no need to fear.

I knew that from the moment of my conception

I had been prepared for this awareness,

For this place,

For this love.

42 Once in a Lifetime

In packing my belongings for my upcoming move,

I came across a love letter.

The words took my breath away.

To be loved like this comes only once in a lifetime.

You can't buy it.

You can't duplicate it.

This kind of love finds you

At the right moment in time.

His words floated off the paper catching my throat.

"Dear Crazy Lady,

Our kind of love, as the song goes,

'Once in my life someone comes along'

Holds so much meaning to me now.

You have been the only person in my life

To accept me as I am.

I wonder why? What do you see?

You are all I have ever desired in a partner.

I question, are you really real

Or is our love just a figment of my imagination?

To be sure,

I have tested you over and over again

To the point that I feared losing you.

I won't promise you a rose garden, but

I will promise to love you the only way I know how.

Fly with me, my beloved into the sunset of our lives."

43 Simple Pleasures

Over the past several years, I remember waking up in the middle of the night to find my husband's head drenched in perspiration.

"Are you okay?" I'd ask. "Your head's dripping wet."

"Yes," Russ would mumble. "It's nothing. Go back to sleep."

We never dreamed those innocent droplets of moisture would lead us down such unchartered waters. Yet we soon found ourselves forging through extremely difficult days that stretched into weeks, then months.

Our journey started November 24, 2008. We had planned to visit my son and his family in Houston, Texas, for Thanksgiving. Russ woke early that morning, once again drenched in perspiration. I wiped his head with a cool damp cloth and after he drank a glass of orange juice, Russ felt fine. No amount of arguing would convince him to postpone our vacation, so off we went.

We arrived safely at my son's home, but each night Russ would awake dripping wet. After downing a 20-ounce power drink and consuming a banana, he'd go right back to sleep. Russ claimed to be okay, but I had my doubts.

During the day, Russ appeared fine. We helped bake Christmas cookies on Monday. Tuesday, we helped decorate their Christmas tree. Wednesday, we opened Christmas gifts, shared memories and just enjoyed being together. Thursday, we celebrated Thanksgiving. Christine, our daughter-in-law, prepared a delicious mouth-watering turkey with all the trimmings. On Friday, after hugs and kisses, Russ and I headed back to Florida.

Once home, the night sweats continued. After two doctor visits in less than four days and a call to EMS one morning when Russ couldn't get out of bed, I ended up taking him to Brandon Hospital. His glucose numbers registered twenty-nine. In minutes, a team of doctors and nurses were asking me all kind of questions.

"Is he diabetic?"

"No!"

"What medicines does Russ take?"

"Here's his list."

"How long has he been sick?"

"About two weeks."

On and on the questions came - *fast and furious* - like water crashing over a cliff.

Nurses drew Russ's blood, technicians connected Russ to monitors, another person shot a large tube of dextrose into his vein, and while one doctor checked Russ's heart and another read the printout. The experience was beyond frightening. Finally, Russ's glucose numbers began to rise only to plummet again. The dextrose just flushed through his system puzzling the doctors.

After weeks of tests, the doctors informed us that Russ had *"a cancerous tumor in his pancreas."* The words exploded like thunder in our ears, rocking our world like a sonic blast. Russ sat in his bed stunned.

Orders to transport Russ to Moffitt Cancer Center were written. Once there, more tests proved Russ has a very rare, extremely aggressive, high-grade, fast-growing neuroendocrine tumor at the head of his pancreas that has metastasized throughout his liver. The doctor immediately ordered aggressive chemotherapy consisting of carboplatin and etoposide.

I called and emailed our friends and family asking for prayers. My friend Jan reminded me of the verse "Cast your cares on the LORD, and he will sustain you; he will never let the righteous be shaken." (Psalm 55:22 NIV). It was much needed encouragement.

Russ's doctor discharged him on New Year's Eve. Home health care monitored him for several weeks. Russ endured continuous testing, scans, shots, and even periodic blood transfusions. The good news showed the chemo was keeping the tumor from growing. The bad news came during our next doctor's appointment.

"You do understand the cancer is incurable?" his doctor asked.

"Yes." We nodded. I had to fight back tears, yet somehow, I managed a smile and squeezed Russ's hand.

Russ endured six series of treatments that involved four trips to Moffitt every twenty-one days before the doctor temporarily discontinued the therapy.

"Your body needs a rest. We'll schedule a scan in two months and see how you're doing. Do you have any questions?"

"No," we said softly.

We agreed Russ's body needed the rest. Our trips to the hospital were sapping both our strengths. The break allowed us some "normal" time together. The weeks raced by until the scheduled appointment was upon us. This time the scan produced good news.

"The cancer appears to be in remission," the doctor explained. "We'll wait three more months, and schedule another scan. I can only guess when it will begin to grow again. You might be able to go without chemo until the end of the year, but I can't promise that."

"Thank you, doctor" could not express the overwhelming gratitude and joy we felt. His gift of six months was an answer to prayer, and the doctor's inability to guarantee the future was not a problem. We were leaving that up to God. Meanwhile, we returned to enjoying life one day at a time.

To ward off fear, I read as much as I could about Russ's cancer. Then one day, I realized knowledge wasn't the key to living with this killer. Scripture held the key to my peace.

I searched for verses offering comfort, strength, and positive reinforcement that God was in control. Slowly I found peace. Not knowing how much time we had left together, our lives changed considerably. The statement "the future is now" became our daily motto.

Over the years, Russ hadn't been the type to tell me he loved me, but now, the words: "I love you," are spoken almost daily. Unlike the past, "Thank you" and "I'm sorry" have become second nature to him.

Kisses no longer are limited to special moments. Russ makes the bed, does dishes, and folds laundry without being asked. Laughter has replaced the tension living in our house. Simple pleasures bring contentment. We are grateful for each day. Cancer redefined the meaning of happiness, and we are making this time some of the best days of our marriage.

When Russ's journey is over, it's only the beginning for him. He will know what we both have believed is really true. Somewhere, in the silence of my nights, I hope to sense Russ encouraging me to stay the course until we are together with the Lord, where all the promises of Jesus truly do flow like living waters. Meanwhile, I trust God's grace will carry us through these rough turbulent times, and He will eventually bring us both safely home.

When times are good, be happy; but when times are bad,
consider this:
God has made the one as well as the other.
Ecclesiastes 7:14 NIV

Edited & Published in Women of the Secret Place

by Ruth Carmichael Ellinger & others

Ambassador International 2012

44 Joy of the Redeemed

Let the eyes of the blind be opened.
Let the ears of the deaf hear.
Let those with feeble hands be strengthened.
Let the lame leap like the deer.

Let those with fearful hearts be encouraged
For ours is the Lord of love
Whose promise to dwell with us always,
Is sealed in the Savior's blood.

Let His great and mighty plans for us
Melt our fears like snow in May.
Let our spirits rejoice in thanksgiving,
As we share His promises today.

45 Celebrate

Hurray! We pray —

for God is good

to all His children

everyday,

loving them,

leading them,

He has planned the Way.

Hurray! We pray —

for Jesus lives

in the hearts of His children

everyday,

loving them,

redeeming them,

He's prepared the Way.

Hurray! We pray —

for the Spirit dwells

within His children

everyday,

loving them,

guiding them,

He preserves the Way,

as He gathers them together

for the true life

come Judgment Day!

For he will command his angels concerning

you to guard you in all your ways.

Psalm 91:11

46 Dawn of Discovery

The early morning light whispers in my ear
as darkness gives way to a new day.

Wake up sleepy head!

You'll miss the sweet music of the song birds, and
the sparkling rainbow droplets on the lilies.

Get up! Get up!

Drink in the peace before the world awakens.
Breathe in the joy waiting for your entrance.

Come see the colors of dawn.
There is time for sleep later.

This pristine canvas has been painted by your maker.
Let its beauty fill your soul.

Oh, foolish person,

Why do you cling to a fleeting second of slumber?

Why do you exchange experiencing God's

masterpiece for sleep?

Open your eyes before this moment vanishes.

This wonder waits for no one.

It comes but once in your lifetime.

Wake up! Wake up!

47 A Toast to the New Year

Antique wine goblets, delicately etched,
Stand at attention.
One full of sweetness and sparkling bubbles,
One simply void of life
Unaware of the coming new year.

Decorative hats and blaring horns
Welcome the unknown.
Gas filled balloons and dancing streamers
Carry dreams of hope upward
As chimes of twelve ring out.

Blackened skies explode with magical fire
Painting tapestries
That takes my breath.
My inner child
Squeals with delight.

Then, I catch a whiff of your scent.

My head jerks, my heart flutters,

My mind struggles to focus.

It cannot be and yet,

I hope beyond hope.

Memories of your laughing eyes,

Your tender embrace,

Wrap themselves around my sadness.

Your love lingers in my heart.

Death took you much too soon.

I sip the nectar of the vine

Accepting time is no longer ours.

I lift my glass

With a sad goodbye,

And cautiously greet the New Year.

"Don't let your hearts be troubled,

Trust in God, and trust also in me."

John 14:1 NLT

48 The Water's Edge

You came into my life
Like waves crashing onto an unsuspecting beach
Washing away the pain of my past.

You propelled me into an unknown world
Filled with laughter, beauty, and the colors of the
rainbow
That I had only dreamed of.

The countless hours of silence shared,
Sitting at the water's edge
Molded us together like sand castles.

Our love reflected the brilliance of the dancing waters
Warming our hearts,
Melting the chill of days gone by.

The intimate moments of passion

That carried us through the rough times

Sealed our love.

Our first twenty-five years challenged the joy

Found only in heaven,

Traveling from sea to shining sea.

Then, like a thief in the night,

Death stole you away and the years dim the

memories

I try desperately to hold onto.

My only solace is knowing your battle is over,

Your struggle to live has ended,

And that you dwell safely in the presence of the

Lord.

So, I watch the sun dip slowly below the water's edge

Leaving behind two empty beach chairs

Filled with a lifetime of bliss.

49 An Unexpected Surprise

Our class reunion produced
an unexpected surprise.

After years of living
in different places,
our lives have reconnected.

As we danced across the floor,
arm in arm,
talking about how we've lived,
and why we parted,
we questioned ourselves, "Why?"

My finger touched your lips,
and I encouraged you
to just enjoy the now.

These are our moments,

a space in time, breathe in.

We can only hope for tomorrow.

and pray the years have not been wasted.

I believe

the time was meant to be

for years apart have been for growing,

for our becoming.

We share what is ours to share,

don't try to write the next paragraph,

don't dream of clouds in the sky.

Stay on solid ground.

Only yesterday knows the ending.

Only tomorrow knows the beginning.

Enjoy the friendship found

after all these years.

Embrace the dance, my friend.

It is ours for the moment.

Drink in the possibilities.

and celebrate being alive.

50 Becoming

What you watch,

What you read,

What you listen to,

What you talk about

is

What you are becoming.

Be wise and set your focus

On what you want to become.

Then, commit both yourself

And your desires to

The Lord Jesus Christ.

Watch

And wait,

See what He has

Planned for your life.

Commit your way to the LORD.

Psalm 37:5 NIV

51 A Place Called Home

Home to me was a place where my parents lived. Their first residence could be found at the top of a steep set of stairs. It consisted of a space adequate for two adults and eventually, two little girls. Actually, the apartment formed the second floor of my grandmother's house in Ottawa, Ohio. The year was 1930. Then mother became pregnant with me forcing us to move as we became packed like sardines in Grandmother's attic.

My family and I lived in a little rented house out in the country for the next few years. It had a red tile roof, two tiny bedrooms, a kitchen with a potbellied stove that would hiss at you if you flicked water on it, and outdoor plumbing. The outhouse had one hole, no toilet paper, as we know it today, and plenty of mean wasps. I don't recall a living room, but there must have been one.

In 1940 Dad got a job at Willy's Overland in Toledo, Ohio, making jeeps for the war effort. We moved first to an apartment and then to a rented house near Lake Erie and finally, in 1942, to a brand-new house in rural East Toledo. By then I was six years old.

Home now had a real kitchen with running water. Mother canned bright colored vegetables, baked steaming hot bread, and fed our hungry family in this wonderful corner of the house. My parents had their own bedroom. My two sisters and I even shared a bedroom all to ourselves. We often gathered in our tiny living room to listen to the latest addition to our home—a stand-up radio. But the best area in the house was the bathroom. No more running outdoors to pee.

The house had a basement that held a coal stove and a play area for us. The temperature remained cool in the summer and warm in the winter. From splatter painting to coloring in what seemed an endless supply of coloring books, we played down there for hours. But dress-up soon became our favorite pastime. Wrapped in

Grandmother's old lace curtains and discarded sheets, we were transformed into fairy princesses and Cinderella. *Home* was heaven.

Six years went by, when once again we hauled the boxes up from the basement. After hours of packing, we made several trips to our new place about seven miles away. But this time, *home* resembled a mansion. The contractor had just finished building it. You could smell the aroma of freshly painted walls and the spicy odor of the wood framing.

The house consisted of four bedrooms, a living room, a large kitchen, one bathroom, and a basement the size of our entire house. Dad eventually put a shower in one corner of the basement that shared space with Mother's washing machine, shelves of her canned goods, a huge coal furnace, and a dirty coal bin. The rest of the basement was designated as our area.

I entered the ninth grade while living in our mansion. Then things began to radically change. Mary Lou, my oldest sister, met a nice young man soon after she graduated from high school. They were married and she moved away. Next, Carole graduated from high school. She too got married and moved away. I worked for a year before I got married at age nineteen.

Being an extremely sensitive person filled with numerous untamed fears, all these changes left me very unsettled.

The first year of our marriage, my husband served in Korea with the Air Force, so I remained with my parents. When he returned, he received orders for a base at Abilene, Texas. *Home* became a small dwelling on the second floor of a building containing seven tiny apartments. The living room became our bedroom at night with a Murphy bed that unfolded from a closet. It had a shotgun kitchen with a tiny built-in booth for eating. Our washing machine sat in the corner hall leaving just enough room to squeeze into the miniature bathroom. I longed for the safety and familiarity of my parent's *home*.

A year and a half later, we moved to Tampa where my husband checked in at MacDill Air Base. We lived on the second floor in a small garage apartment, nothing really to talk about, unless you consider discovering disgustingly ugly Palmetto bugs in my house. I also had a small stove in the kitchen that wasn't grounded correctly, and it gave me a shock each time I used it.

Next, he got stationed in Baffin Island northeast of Maine for a year, so I moved back in with my parents who had just purchased a new home in Bradenton, Florida. Once again, I felt safe.

Our son, David, was born in November while I lived with my parents. When my husband returned to the States the following February, he had orders for a base in South Dakota. Off we went to the frozen north. We rented a nice sized duplex apartment in the country, only to discover it was poorly insulated. Forty-two degrees below zero was a far cry from sunny Florida.

Thankfully, two and a half years later, we returned to the Sunshine State. I had saved enough money to put a down payment on my parent's house as they were in the process of having a new home built. Don, my husband, had six months to go before he would finish his duty. His last station was in Eagle Pass, Texas. *Home* there was a little rented house that had Black Widows in the attic and little furniture. I couldn't wait to return to Bradenton and begin living a normal life.

Home soon consisted of a large living room, a dining room, a super kitchen lined with cupboards, one bathroom, two bedrooms, a back porch, and a single car garage. We settled in only to move again four years later to Brandon, Florida, due to my husband changing jobs. By then our daughter, Doreen, had been born. We rented a house until the place we would finally call home was finished being constructed. I just knew this would be where I would live out the rest of my life.

Home welcomed you into an entrance hall that opened into a beautiful living room. It was connected to a formal dining room with a door that led to the kitchen with more cupboards. A small family room opened to a long hall where a large bathroom and three bedrooms could be found. The master bedroom even had its own bathroom. This felt like home. But it was not to be.

A divorce forced the sale of the house, and I took my children to yet another apartment building, small but adequate. My son, David, graduated from high school and joined the Army. I remarried in 1978.

Russell, my new husband, and I moved into a nice used house that had been well cared for. *Home* now had a large living room with a bay window in the front, a formal dining room, a long hall that opened to three bedrooms and two baths. It contained another shotgun kitchen that led to an eating area, a large family room, a screened-in back porch, and a double car garage. After a couple of years, my daughter decided she wanted to live with her father, so she left. *Home* was way more than two people needed, but we entertained our family and friends for years in what I considered my last *home*. Wrong again.

Just before Russell was due to retire, he had open-heart surgery, my father died, and I relocated my mother a few miles from us to a mobile home in Feather Rock in Valrico. Russell worried if he had a heart attack and died, how would I manage? Concerned for my safety, we sold our house and moved one last time into a gated community called Strawberry Ridge in Valrico, Florida. Mother was now only two miles from us.

We picked out a new Palm Harbor manufactured home comparable in size to our house we had just left except with a carport instead of a garage. Therefore, we had a small building attached to the house for Russell's tools, my washer and dryer, and our newly purchased golf cart. Then we had another room built on the other end of the house, next to the screened porch, to hold his large lawn mower, garden tools, Christmas decorations, and whatever found their way into the shed. For the next fourteen years this has been called *home*, and it has served us well.

Unfortunately, my mother passed away in 2003 and Russell died in 2010. I hesitate to say this would be my last *home* before heaven because I have been mistaken before.

Then, in 2017, Hurricane Irma raced through the center of the state causing all kinds of havoc. Fears for my safety caused my son to bring me to Boerne, Texas, near him. *Home* is now a two-bedroom, two baths, living room, dining area, and a nice sized kitchen apartment. Downsizing required me to give away many of my possessions. Strangely, it came easy and now I am all but settled in calling this *home*.

Contentment has become my partner these days, and joy and peace fill my apartment *home* as I slowly transform it to reflect my personality. I have learned a house is just a place with four walls and a roof, but *home* is where my spirit flourishes nurturing my creativity and love for life. I have no doubt God will provide a dwelling place for me that I can finally call *home* as I travel through my final years. Meanwhile, I fill my days to the fullest with His unlimited blessings.

52 A Dream in a Chosen Place

Assemble a group of like-minded believers,

People of the Living God.

Find the land God has set aside

For His Glory.

Teach the Word,

Receive the sacraments,

Grow in faith

And watch the Holy Spirit move,

Often, too slowly for some.

Fuel the dream not all can see.

Stay focused on the Cross.

Catch the vision,

As God provides the few

Needed to complete the heart's desire.

Sadly, Satan cleverly picked away

at the foundation

until the dream imploded within its walls.

Believers scatter, yet a handful remain

To finish the work God had called

Them to do.

Recalling the procession that carried the

Crosses, the candles, the altar linens, and

The Holy Scriptures

Into the small sanctuary,

Tears fell in joy.

For now,

The procession carries

The crosses, the candles, the altar linens, and

The Holy Scriptures

Out of the small sanctuary

And hearts break.

A bittersweet journey

Of a dream,

Gone awry,

Comes to an end.

The doors are locked

And the believers are

Scattered.

Yet,

God's work had been done

In this chosen place.

53 Our Best

From the tiniest seed

Comes the smallest weed,

Or a giant tree, no less.

For it's what we plant,

Not what we can't,

That gives God glory best!

54 Called Back to Heaven

My friend has died,

I cried.

Words of comfort spoken,

many hearts broken.

An angel called back to heaven.

Her time too short,

but what a sport.

Always helping,

truly amazing.

An angel called back to heaven.

How blessed to know

a living rainbow,

shared love so kind,

totally color-blind,

An angel called back to heaven.

A job well-done,

leaving a daughter and son.

And a husband so true.

We'll sadly miss you,

Sweet angel called back to heaven.

55 The Desert Miracle

"Time for the news, honey," my husband called.

"Okay. I'll be there in a moment."

Eventually I settled into my chair when a short clip on television showed an inconceivable event that had occurred in the Iraqi war that day. For thirty seconds, my mind stood still. Then, several meaningless commercials filled the screen, followed by the local news, and yet, my memory wouldn't let go of the incredible pictures I had observed moments earlier.

Tick tock, tick tock

The hands on my grandfather clock continued their circle, but I seemed frozen, unable to move past the unbelievable events my eyes had witnessed. Somehow the news story had transported me to the Iraqi desert, like a mouse hiding in a tank taking in all the action, firsthand.

Tick tock, tick tock

The year was 2003, orders had been given to 50,000 American military personnel to storm the desert and take control of Baghdad. Pushing forward, they encountered winds that could be classified only as Brown Out. Sand stung their faces, attacking their eyes and ears. Their mouths filled with the grit.

The soldiers scrambled to protect their fragile high-tech equipment from the havoc the tiny grains of flying matter could incur. Desert training was mandatory before being sent to Iraq, but they weren't prepared for these extremely intense conditions.

Muslim communities from around the world called it a *Divine Wind — a gift from Allah* to bring the infidels to their knees. The sandstorm raged on for three days, carrying the lethal pellets across the desert floor, winning the record as the most violent sandstorm in 100 years.

Without a warning, the winds vanished but were quickly replaced by a driving rainstorm. The horrendous downpour drenched the area multiplying the suffering. Our news media predicted gloom and doom, while Christians around the world prayed for the troop's safety.

Tick tock, tick tock

Then, like in the eye of a hurricane, all went still and the sun appeared. Yet our mighty war machine stood silent, astounded at what lay before them. A frightening gasp echoed throughout the stalled tanks. Just inches away thousands upon thousands of anti-tank and antipersonnel mines could be seen scattered across the desert floor. The winds and rains had uncovered their hiding places, revealing the death trap the Iraqi army had set. The devastation would have been unbelievable.

My heart ached as tears streamed down my face. God had been more than faithful in answering the prayers for our troops. For now, the soldiers were safe, and we praised God for the miraculous way He delivered them from pending disaster.

Tick tock, tick tock

The memory of those television commercials has long been covered with the sands of time, yet those *thirty seconds of electrifying truth* remain forever etched in my mind. I can still picture God's desert miracle, and how He protected our army from certain doom in the land of the desert sun.

Tick tock, tick tock

56 The Sly Young Fox

Straight Arrow was special right from birth,
Wide eyed, with a captivating smile,
And clever beyond his days.
He grew fast, and strong,
And remembered all he saw,

He was open to knowledge and studied hard,
Developing a keen sense of right and wrong.
He worked diligently to hone his skills.
Pain proved to be no hindrance,
Nor did the lack of comfort.

Fear never played a role in his life,
Nothing kept him from his goal.
His unquenchable desire for adventure,
Led him into leadership where he achieved much,
Duty and honor were never to be questioned.

Then, one day, he met his downfall.

Her bronze body shimmered in the sunlight.

Jet-black hair cascaded down her shoulders,

And when she turned around,

Her beauty took his breath.

She was tall, but not too tall,

He imagined her fitting right under his arm.

Her smile and laughter mesmerized him.

He became relentless in his pursuit,

She would be his!

But, she showed no special interest in him.

A polite smile at a joke or two,

Then she'd turn and go on her way.

Her simple manner and trusting spirit,

He felt, was no match for his clever mind.

So, Straight Arrow devised his perfect trap.

First, he sent out his brothers, one by one,

To test her honor,

And each time, they returned without a trophy.

She was not to be had.

Small talk and unexpected meetings,
Fostered his love for her.
Working together on common projects
Linked their lives, until one day
She offered her hand in friendship.

He knew his cunning trap had worked.
But, unbeknownst to him, she loved him too.
Somehow, someday, she knew that he would be hers.
All she had to do was wait, and slowly reel him in.

And that is how the quiet beauty
Skillfully outsmarted the sly young fox.

57 Darkness

Called out of darkness
into the light.
Coaxed out of darkness
to God's own delight.
Guided out of darkness
His mercy receive.
Conqueror of darkness
when you believe.

Called out of darkness
Into the light,
Coaxed out of darkness
He gives you new sight.
Guided out of darkness
a chosen few.
Conqueror of darkness
now includes you.

Called out of darkness

into the light.

Coaxed out of darkness

our forces unite.

Guided out of darkness

Enhance the flame.

Conqueror of darkness

His message proclaims!

The people walking in darkness

have seen a great light.

Isaiah 9:2 NIV

58 A Gentle Wind

When the doors to the garden flew open,

Eve lost her way.

The sweet juices of sin

Fleeced her innocence

And virtues quickly became passé.

Time amassed generations of the blind.

The Rule Book collected dust.

Consequences dissolved in darkness,

Silencing the protesters,

Replacing courtship with lust.

Roguish voices tickled the ears of the lost.

Preaching tolerance as the truth.

Yet a gentle wind whispered to their souls,

Return to me and know the joy

Of the glory days of youth.

Their struggles persisted like a mighty storm,

The winds of summer lost no time.

In desperation, they cried aloud,

And the hand of healing restored their lives

Washing away layers and layers of grime.

Yet, the battle continued day after day,

But the armor of God protected their souls.

His promises sure to those who believe

In Christ Jesus, their mighty Lord,

Whose gift of forgiveness overflows.

The garden, once perfect, remains amiss,

While spiritual evil continues to deride.

But the sweet love of their Savior

And His powerful Word

Stands guard daily protecting His Bride.

59 Incredible Gifts

Life today is far different than when I first met Jesus. Not having been raised a Christian, my fear followed me closer than my shadow. Undetected dyslexia didn't help my struggle to find a level path, and pride engulfed my heart like a stream after a heavy spring rain. A perfect performance didn't bring peace, and I knew nothing of grace. I was in desperate need of the Savior.

My journey to the Father's house looks like a road map gone awry; two steps forward, four back. My first memory of hearing about Jesus came from the bedtime prayer: *Now I lay me down to sleep. If I should die* sent shivers down my spine, bringing little comfort to my youthful ears.

By my ninth birthday, my two sisters and I walked to a little Methodist church to attend Sunday school. Our teacher gave each of us a Bible. The contents were very mysterious, and the print extremely tiny. Excitement bubbled inside me.

Then the teacher said we had to memorize the names of the books in order to receive a small plastic cross that glowed in the dark. My heart turned heavy as no one at home could pronounce all the names let alone help me memorize them. I abruptly quit her class.

Several years later, a neighbor took the three of us a few times to the First Congregational Church in Ottawa Hills where she worshipped. People dropped twenty-dollar bills in a silver plate that was passed around. I couldn't believe it. Mother only got that much for a week's worth of groceries for the six of us.

Then in 1951, I watched a story about Jesus with my sisters on television. When Christ was nailed to the cross, I cried. My sisters chased me out of the room. Therefore, I didn't learn about His resurrection. That year, my mother took us to church for Easter services. I thought my heart would explode; the worship was so exciting. She agreed to take us to Christmas Eve services too.

The next three years, we became *CE* Christians. (Christmas Easter)

After graduating from high school, I worked in the Toledo Public Library, got married at nineteen, and spent the next year waiting for my husband to return from duty in Korea. One of my fellow workers asked me if I was baptized.

"No," I said, embarrassed that I didn't even know what that meant.

She called me a heathen. I wanted to crawl under my desk. But God in His infinite wisdom had a plan. When my husband returned to the US, his orders sent us to Abilene, Texas. Amazingly, our landlord's father was a Methodist minister. One day he spoke to me about this mysterious thing called baptism.

"Would you like me to baptize you?" he asked.

"Oh, would you?" A few days later, Christ claimed me as His child.

Next, we were stationed in South Dakota where we attended a Lutheran Church. I went through extensive study and was eventually confirmed. I met a group of Presbyterian women who taught me about prayer. I knew then that I had arrived. Baptized, confirmed, membership, and now prayer; what more could there be? The answer took years to discover.

Hours of Bible study, repeated sins, constant forgiveness, relinquishing of fear, surrender of pride, divorce, and finally, a Christian husband—all incredible gifts from our Lord. Strangely, life became harder instead of easier, but slowly God opened my eyes.

Through study, service, and seeking His narrow path, God replaced my past with a joyous present and the promise of a magnificent future in His glorious kingdom. It has been a long arduous journey, but well worth the effort.

This is what the LORD says: . . . "For I know the plans I have for you,"

declares the LORD, "plans to prosper you and not to harm you,

plans to give you hope and a future."

Jeremiah 29:10–11 NIV

60 Beginning Anew

It's so hard to lose my mother,
To have said goodbye to dad,
The love they shared kept me strong,
When I was just a tad.

They seemed to know just what to say,
The comfort they did share,
His words so firm, her touch so soft,
The loss I cannot bear.

And yet, I'm told it's not goodbye,
We're all just passing through,
This troubled world, we'll leave behind,
If only I truly knew.

O Lord, my God, if you're real indeed,
Don't let me struggle so.
The pain is deep, the sorrow dark,

But then, You already know.

I've looked away from wisdom taught,

And closed my heart to hope.

Please lift me up and open my eyes

So, I no longer have to grope.

Your Word they taught to me each day,

They believed with all their heart.

I want that Lord, I truly do,

Please give me a fresh new start.

My sins out-number the grains of sand

On all the beaches You've made.

My burdens heavy, my body weak,

My mind completely frayed.

The truth Dad taught, the hope Mom gave

Wells up in me anew.

I sense Your peace; I feel Your love,

My struggle I give to You.

How foolish I've been to try alone
While You stood standing there,
With all your promises waiting for me
To receive and freely share.

So, I say goodbye to my mother dear,
My father long has passed,
Knowing this pain was for my growth,
You've set me free at last.

How can I thank You Lord, my God
For all Your mercy shown.
Take my life and lead the way,
Your story I will make known.

61 Time Shared

Your knock woke me from a deep sleep.
I found you standing at my door
with empty hands
and wide eyes filled with pain.
I invited you in.

We embraced, my friend, becoming one.
I received your confession;
extending grace once given me.

In you, I saw myself in years past,
full of questions
trying to navigate
what is real, what is right,
what is truth.

Walking through the gardens
of our memories,

reminded us how seeds become
what they were designed to be.
Some bushes, some weeds,
some beautiful flowers
all reaching to the light.

Hopefully, time shared
displaced some of the darkness,
some of the lies you tell yourself.

Wisdom is a process,
my fragile friend,
often confusing, but worth the effort
like the short life
of the elegant butterfly,
once freed of the struggle,
performs its dance of life.

We each have been chosen
by our Maker for a purpose.
Trust Him with the process, and fly.

May the God of hope fill you with all joy and peace, as you

trust in Him,

so that you may overflow with hope by the power of the

Holy Spirit.

Romans 15:13 NIV

62 The Dance Within

Can you see it? Do you hear the music?

Can you feel the rhythm flowing in my veins?

This freedom is new to me,

ever changing, always the same.

The chemistry demands total commitment.

An unknown force carries me forward,

leaping into waiting arms of another.

We move as one.

Time multiplies.

Droplets of moisture congregate.

My body ignores exhaustion.

On and on, my arms stretch and recoil.

My body folds, then flips. Muscles flex.

I press on,

spinning, twisting, tumbling gracefully.

Ebb and flow create an allusion

of elegant simplicity.

Powerful scores control

the very essence of my nature.

I have become the dance.

63 In the Nick of Time

It was Tuesday, the 29th of June, a day for celebrating my younger sister's birthday. For some women, becoming thirty-seven would be depressing, but for Bobbie it was a very special time in her life. With her recent marriage to Jeff, she had all but forgotten the disappointment of her past marriages. I saw Jeff as truly a blessing sent by God. Although I would not be able to be with them, I felt their joy and thanked God for their happiness.

Turning my thoughts from that joy, ones of sadness took their place as I faced the reason why I wouldn't be with them. My father was fighting a losing battle with cancer, and the decision of visiting him today had to be made.

It wasn't a difficult drive, only fifty miles down the interstate, but I struggled with the question should I go today or wait till tomorrow? I was so tired. Life had been dealing me an unlimited amount of opportunities lately, but the fact that my father hadn't received Jesus as his Savior yet, kept coming to the forefront of my mind.

Dad was so stubborn. I had always thought that was where my sisters and I had gotten our strong natures, until I become a Christian. Poor Dad, how he had wanted a boy, and all he had gotten was four little girls. How disappointed he had been.

As I sat there, I wondered what other disappointments he held inside that we would never know now that he was near the end of his life.

Our visits these last few months had been very revealing, even painful at times. We talked about the needs both of us had had but never dealt with. We laughed at good times remembered and cried about some of our hurts. We shared secrets that we had never felt safe to share before. The limited time element seemed to cut through the normal small talk, and at last, it opened up the doorway allowing honesty to be shared between my father and me.

Like many families who survived the Great Depression, we hadn't had a lot of things, but my parents usually had a garden, and the shelves in the basement were always filled with interesting looking things Mother had canned. She also sewed most of our clothes, which helped stretch dad's paycheck. I'll never forget the time spent playing games at the kitchen table. He never let us win, unless we deserved to. And how he loved to tease. I told him how it hurt me.

"You were such a sensitive kid," he said. "I'm sorry." We both cried.

Dad received Jesus into his heart just weeks before he died.

64 Ode to My Happy Clown

Hi there Mrs. Clown.

You seem really happy today.

All dressed for a party I see.

Whose birthday are we celebrating?

Your curly hair looks like someone

Colored it with a rainbow.

And what can I say about those baggy pants?

Are you hiding some toys in them?

Speaking of hiding, thanks for becoming.

I have been waiting a long time for you.

Who would have guessed you were waiting

Inside of me, too.

Sometimes it takes life to create loving people.

I'm glad we have finally become friends.

Funny, how sadness can make for a happy clown.

You have helped me walk those hospital halls

And bring smiles to oodles of hurting patients.

It is strange how healing comes in all different ways.

Who would have guessed it could come through me

as a happy clown?

65 Ode to My Inner Mime

I see you finally showed up.

Where have you been all my life?

Why did it take so long for you to materialize?

You pretend to be shy and hide behind your mask.

Always fidgeting, doing silly antics.

Speak up,

Mime.

I can't hear you.

Quit pretending to cry,

acting as if I hurt your feelings.

How do you think I feel?

I have waited a long time

for you to make your appearance.

This is serious stuff.

Yet, you never add to our conversation.

Deep inside me

I always knew you were there.

Trust me,

Don't be afraid to be different.

Reach out and embrace life.

Welcome to my world.

Oh, one more thing,

could you change your outfit once in a while?

66 Goals and Aspirations

I know,

That deadlines force my focus,

But they also create stress.

Finding the middle ground is critical,

If I am to write my very best.

Therefore,

If I am to master the written word,

I must devour the book of truth.

Where words explain words

with even more words

So, I am able to write with less.

Consequently,

Catching the memories before they're gone,

While maintaining my normal life,

Is a trick that I, indeed, must learn,

So, my family and friends and I, myself,

Don't get lost in the process and protest!

So,

What are my goals and aspirations,

Seeing you've given me only a week to think?

Praying for a miracle

to stretch the time,

Motivation to write stories

Instead of playing with rhyme,

Finding the balance in all that I do,

Being intentional, but playful too,

Enjoying the now, while I write the past,

Sharing this gift so that it will last,

If I can learn how to do all this,

Then, miracle upon miracle,

I will have learned how to write

My very best!

67 The Voice of Love

To say my life has always been lived on the sunny side of the street is an exaggeration. My happy smile and lighthearted spirit of today reflects little, if any, of the fear, anxiety, depression, and even an attempted suicide that found their way into my former life. My faith in God resembled a bungee cord of unpredictability with its ups and downs keeping me off balance. Darkness stalked me, hiding behind my persona of being in control.

Then out of thin air, it happened.

I was elected to sit on our district's board of churchwomen. The next event would be a retreat in Sarasota, Florida. Ringling Brothers headquarters resides there, so the board decided the decorations, theme and Saturday evening banquet would reflect the celebration of the clown. Each board member was instructed to create a clown outfit to wear for the evening to add to the festivities. I knew little about clowning, but with a friend's help, I pulled together a costume. The event launched my calling into the world of clowning.

Several months later, I attended a *gospel clown* workshop offered by a nearby church. Choosing the right costume proved more difficult than I imagined, but the sensitivity training for clowning really surprised me. The instructor explained the connection between love and sacrifice with clowns and how you give up your identity once your costume is complete.

"Clowning is serious business," he said, "especially gospel clowning."

He helped me choose a design and showed me how to apply the oil paint to my face. Next, the breath-catching powder that was used to set the oils flew everywhere creating an unbelievable mess. Colorful balloons, fuzzy hand puppets, and silly noisemakers were handed out.

I embraced with zeal the serious business of playing. Unfortunately, the day ended much too soon, but something inside me said this event was just the beginning of things to come. But what?

Once again, I fought with depression caused by the unwarranted firing from my job as an office manager in a large financial firm. The darkness threatened to overwhelm me. Then that strange feeling I experienced at the church stirred in me again.

Ideas exploded as how to build on the knowledge I had obtained at the clowning event. The thoughts weren't mine. They angered my husband when I shared them with him. He feared I was losing my mind.

Yet within weeks, I had chosen a name: Bette, The Imaginary Clown. I sewed three outfits, purchased a rainbow-colored wig, designed a business card, and painted an old suitcase bright yellow trimmed in red. I filled it with all kind of magical things. The feeling kept me moving forward.

I designed a green fuzzy hand puppet with big dark eyes and long brown eyebrows. I gave it the name of Bashful Bette. The children would eventually love her. I sewed a furry yellow duck with a pointed head, a large mouth that opened and closed, black button eyes, and two red legs, each fifteen inches long. Naturally his name had to be Silly Duck. He too would become a favorite of the children. There was a large green frog; a magic wand, which was an old car antenna; a book whose pictures would disappear; a narrow green plastic groan tube; and so much more.

Being a left-brain person, my husband couldn't understand my actions and begged me to stop. His disapproval came at me like a raging thunderstorm, yet it couldn't dampen my plans. My endorphin levels rose dramatically. He feared for my mental health, and I must admit, once again, I questioned my sanity as well. Where were these ideas coming from? And where would they lead me? It didn't take long to discover the answer.

A friend asked me to do her child's birthday party. I eagerly responded that the Happy Clown would be thrilled to entertain the children. We agreed on a price, but still my husband wasn't convinced.

On the day of the event, I smeared the white oil all over my face, dusted it with powder, added the details, pulled on my wig of rainbow-colored curls and slipped into my bright colored suit. Upon leaving my bedroom, I glanced into the mirror. To my surprise there was no identifying with the person looking back at me.

At that moment, what our instructor had tried to warn us about became clear. I had lost myself in becoming a clown and was free to be whatever I chose. The tremendous responsibility it posed caught in my throat.

As time went by, I walked in the 4th of July parade, visited children in the hospital, and attended charity events. I created another character called my Crazy Lady clown who did Workshops for Women, speaking on numerous subjects, helping other women to laugh, to face down depression, and to rise up free to move forward with their lives.

I mimed for a class of autistic children at a local elementary school. Their struggles to exist reminded me of the prison of my past. My ministry continued to expand taking on still another identity — that of *The Gospel Clown.*

I created a black and white suit with large red pom-poms, a tight-fitting cap, long white gloves, and dancing slippers. All that was needed was a cross to wear around my neck. It had to be special, but how, and where would I find it?

On my way home from shopping one day, I got that strange feeling again. It said, "Pull into this strip mall." I ignored it. The feeling became stronger. "Pull into this strip mall," it prompted. Looking at the stores, I saw nothing of interest. "Pull into this strip mall," it thundered in my head. I quickly obeyed.

Walking past several shops, nothing caught my attention. Then the feeling said, "Go in here." I didn't hesitate. A clerk stepped forward and asked if she could help me find something. I told her of my need for a unique cross.

"I have just the thing for you," she said. "It has a little stain on it, but silver polish will clear it up. You need to understand all sales are final as we are closing our business tomorrow."

I gasped as she handed me the item. It was a heart the size of a silver dollar with a cement nail down through the middle of the charm. As she tried to remove the spot, a deep red color appeared on the metal that looked like a bloodstain. I knew instantly it was why I was led into this store.

I quickly paid her and rushed to my car before my legs gave out from under me. Tears streamed down my face as I sat gazing at the heart, a heart that would hang around the neck of my *Gospel Clown* representing the love and sacrifice of my Lord.

I have often wondered: Who was the voice in my head guiding me throughout these experiences? Who gave me the courage to be so different? And what was their purpose? I pose my questions for you to ponder, for you to decide, but I believe it was the same one who walked with me through the darkness and brought me into new life. I truly believe it was the voice of my Lord, the voice of love.

68 The Happy Clown

Can you believe it?

I actually did it.

I left myself behind

In the bathroom mirror

And became a happy clown.

I had rainbow curls

And bold-colored stripes

And feet a mile long,

When the music began

By the marching band,

I followed them right into town.

The high-pitched squeals

And wiggly hands

Came reaching out to me.

They drew me in

We shared our love

And we danced

Around and around.

Like life itself,

It ended much too soon

And I'll never be the same,

All because I dared to share

The day as a happy clown.

Shout for joy to the LORD, all the earth.

Worship the LORD with gladness;

come before him with joyful songs."

Psalm 100:1–2 NIV

69 Over a Cup of Tea

How can I ever tell you
How much you have meant to me?
Your door was always open
Whenever I'd just pop by,
The welcome mat said, "Come on in"
For no reason, rhyme, or why.

You'd quickly brew a pot of tea
Filling delicate china cups.
Then, adding a plate of fresh baked cookies,
As if you knew I'd soon appear,
Leading me into your warm little kitchen,
"Come sit and rest, my dear."

We were like two young innocent girls
Sharing stories of our lives.
Yet, I was all of seventy-one
And you'd soon be eighty-eight.

Lives rich in blessings from our God
Who constantly filled our plate.

I loved the times you shared your tales,
Of family joys and sorrow.
A newborn child, of sickness, death,
And Christmas gatherings beyond belief,
You bubbled over with love unbridled,
Our laughter brought relief.

You patiently listened to all my tales
Of victories and defeats.
A story written, of beads restrung,
And troubles that engulfed my day.
We'd solved the problems of the world
And then I'd go about my way.

The years have brought you wisdom's best,
Resting sweetly in your soul.
A friendship treasured, enriching my life
Beyond all words, His gift to me —
Your open arms, your gentle smile,

All this we've shared over a cup of tea.

70 The Vacancy

There's a little girl at my front window,
Tap, tap, tapping a friendly hello,
With big brown eyes and a happy smile,
She has come to spend some time with me.

I think of all the fun we've shared,
From little girl squeals to precious hugs,
The drying of tears and the bumps I kissed,
Oh, the joy of watching her grow.

The sewing of special dresses so sweet
To learning to pray and creative be,
She was indeed a Mother's Day dream come true.

And then, one day this gift I held,
This soul I loved beyond my own,
This beautiful child a part of me was gone.

Oh, I know, it's not really her
Tapping on my window pane.

But the haunting memories she left behind,
That never seems to leave my mind.

The lovely yellow butterfly she gave,
The stone art, the drawings and the vacancy in my
heart,
All these are stored neatly in a secret place,
Wrapped in tears that don't erase,
Those precious memories so dear to me.

Those memories of the months that she
Was locked safely inside of me,
Almost ten and seven days were they.

Then out she came a treasured joy,
This blessed child I long to hold,
To whom I gave her life and breath,
With no thoughts of how and when
She would take flight and not return.

Oh God, the struggle of letting go,
I question how things went so wrong.

When acts of kindness twisted be,
With truth and meanings so long forgotten,
So much pleasure denied.
So much precious time lost.

Love and forgiveness have no place
In this for me for she withholds all grace.

I pray someday she will return,
To wipe away my tears and pain,
To once more laugh and talk and say,
"Mother, I love you more each day."

I know it's all in God's loving hands,
His grace so comforting to know,
That His will determines the time and place,
If we should meet again.

I press my face against the glass,

In hopes to see those big brown eyes

Looking back at me with tender love,

Ready to fill the space left vacant,

So many, many long years ago.

71 Ocala's Offering

An explosion of brilliant light
streaked across the sky
announcing an impending storm.
Within minutes, heaven's wrath opened.
Our windshield wipers proved useless
against white rain blocking our view.
Ferocious winds did their best
to push us off course.
My husband clung to the steering wheel
struggling to keep us in our lane.
Taillights appeared off in the distance
only to be discovered inches away.
I cried out to God for our safety.
Then, for a moment, the rain subsided.
An exit ramp appeared
Providing an escape from eminent dangers
Interstate driving holds during a violent storm.
Inching our way down a hill,

a gas station stood as a lighted beacon of hope offering us safe harbor. We huddled together under their canopy and waited for friendlier skies.

72 Joy Unfolding

When love bloomed fresh
upon the vine
And joy freely expressed itself,
Eyes contained a thousand dreams,
Smiles spoke volumes in blissful silence,
And gentle words tumbled softly from grateful
hearts.

When love bloomed fresh
upon the vine
And joy freely expressed itself,
Each moment together nourished our souls,
Each day evolved into a wondrous event,
And life contained untold mysteries to embrace.

When love bloomed fresh
upon the vine
And joy freely expressed itself,

Sitting quietly together a breath apart,

Watching dancing stars in pitch of night,

Filled longing hearts with healing balm.

When love bloomed fresh

upon the vine

And joy freely expressed itself,

Shared stories and secrets made us one,

Laughter a king we faithfully served,

And life resonated with beauty beyond control.

When love bloomed fresh

upon the vine

And joy freely expressed itself,

Hearts were unprepared for graying skies,

And the thundering storms that would crush our

love,

Sending withered blossoms sadly to the ground.

Now,

love no longer blooms fresh

upon the vine

And joy struggles to express itself,

As music played is no longer heard,

Sunlight is covered with grasses green,

And two have become one

in the evening dawn.

And so alone

I sit in thought

Embracing the joy

of memories shared,

Thankful for the time

our lives entwined,

When love bloomed fresh

upon the vine

And joy freely expressed itself.

Restore to me the joy of your salvation

and grant me a willing spirit, to sustain me.

Psalm 51:12 NIV

73 Hidden Objects

My late husband worked for the Federal Bureau of Investigation (FBI), and believed in keeping valuables under lock and key. He installed an alarm system in our home, a double lock on our garage door, and a motion detector in our house.

Not to be outdone, I learned to hide things of value around the house when we were gone. Under my dresser seemed like a safe place. On the top shelf in our closet in an old purse was another. And I figured no one would discover the hundred dollar bills I hoarded in the toe of an old pair of shoes in the back of my closet. Just call me Mrs. FBI of the twentieth century.

I did misplace a pair of antique earrings belonging to my great-grandmother one year for several weeks. I put my passport in the jacket pocket of my dress suit. That took a couple of months to find.

Hiding valuables became a dangerous habit until we purchased a computer. My husband created a folder entitled, *Hidden Objects*. He instructed me to type the name of the article and where I had hidden the item and save it in the file. This procedure worked until he died in 2010. Overwhelmed with the workload of being single, I became lax about following his rules.

Fast forward.

In 2014, I made reservations to fly to my son's home in Houston, Texas, for a week. Collecting my prized jewelry, pictures, and papers, I drove to the bank and locked them in my safety deposit box.

The morning of my departure found the house spotless. My To-Do List had been checked and rechecked. My bags were all packed resting at the front door.

I took my shower, got dressed, and opened my jewelry box for a pair of earrings. Like the blazing sun in midsummer, the diamond ring my great-aunt Pearl had given me years ago shot out.

"Oh no!" I yelled. "How did I miss you? You should be in the bank."

There was no time to go put it in the safety deposit box, so I hid it.

"No big deal," I thought. "I'll just record where I've hidden you in the file." Unfortunately, the computer had already been shut down, and no time remained to reboot it. So I repeated over and over again the ring's hiding place, reassuring me that it was locked in my memory — so I thought.

What is the big deal, you ask? Well, the diamond was about a half carat. Because it was so old, about eighty-five years, it also was a deep cut diamond. Mr. Martin, my local jeweler, had reset the diamond in a beautiful whimsical gold setting of smaller diamonds and rubies.

The ring, valued at more than sixteen hundred dollars, was a cherished treasure promised to my granddaughter, Shelby.

"If my memory fails me," I prayed, "I know the ring will reappear eventually."

Upon returning home, I forgot about my ring. Months later, I went to put it on. The ring was nowhere to be found. I searched and searched. Nothing!

Then, like a bolt of lightning, the idea hit me that the ring may have been in the shoes or the jacket I gave to Goodwill.

Scenario after scenario played in my mind. I cried, how could I have been so careless? Stupidity didn't even define my actions. When my son came to visit, months later, he helped me search for the ring. Still nothing! After a good cry, I decided the ring was gone, so I told myself, "Get over it!"

This morning, to my surprise, I pulled a bracelet out of my jewelry box that I seldom wear. Out popped the ring. Who would have believed? It had been there all the time.

I have decided, no more hide and seek for me. No more being Mrs. FBI for this lady.

You want my stuff; go for it.

74 An Autumn Secret

My dearest friend,

as autumn approaches,

I'm so aware of her message

because you taught me how to listen with my heart.

Oh, how I miss you.

As I walk alone, I suddenly sense your presence.

The wisdom that you shared so freely

seems to snuggle close around me

offering protection from the fall winds.

With the spontaneity of a child,

these cool breezes playfully caress my face

and toss my hair about.

They bounce through the grass,

pushing the golden-brown leaves out of my path

only to return to me more briskly

sending shivers down my spine

instantly robbing me of all of my warmth.

But not really.

For deep inside of me there is now

a different kind of warmth,

one that withstands all fall winds,

an inner warmth fed by the spirit of God.

You see, my friend,

as autumn calls out to me

to come see what new secrets she has to reveal.

I praise God for our friendship.

For you opened my eyes to a new way of life,

And now I too, walk with God.

75 The View

A rest stop at the beach finds me two stories up
giving me a panoramic view of the waters below and
a much too busy highway next to my condo.

Unpacking my car,
seven trips up twenty-eight steps,
carrying too much stuff in the afternoon heat,
found me crashed on the couch.

Once I was fully recovered,
out came my paper, pens and laptop.
Over the next seven days,
incident after incident, found their way
recorded in one form or another.

A young man in a red sports car,
while stopped for the traffic light,
looked up and saw me sitting on my porch.

He smiled, waved and yelled up to me,

"You've got the best view in town."

I smiled, waved back and said,

"You've got that right!"

He smiled again and moved on.

It seemed every fifth car on the street below

was a convertible or expensive sports car. I counted

seven corvettes, several sport Mercedes, three Mini

Coopers,

a number of BMW's, a white sport Lexus and two

red Porsches.

All I could think was they shouldn't be near this salt

air.

One little blue beauty was so small

the man's knees were against his chest.

Oh, what man will do to impress people.

One evening as the sun dipped into the gulf,

another young man, badly inebriated,

came staggering by.

Mumbling to himself, he staggered into the street

and back to the sidewalk.

He waved to the traffic and then, wandered back into

the street.

He seemed oblivious to the danger awaiting him.

Finally, he fell to the ground and laid there

for at least ten minutes.

Slowly, he sat up, ran his hands

through his hair, buttoned his shirt,

pulled himself to his feet

and hailed the free trolley.

Fortunately for him, they let him board.

The next day as I was enjoying my walk along the

water's edge,

I took notice of numerous young ladies strolling

along, strutting might

be a better word, donned in their adorable tiny

bikinis. Back and forth

up and down the beach they went. I don't think I was

ever that thin.

Well, maybe.

Young men followed their every move.

One man was so oiled down his body glistened. I

couldn't figure out

who was trying to impress who,

I appeared to be the oldest person on the beach.

There were families with wagons spilling over with

beach toys.

Children covering each other with wet sand while

others

found enjoyment in making sand castles, splashing in

the surf

and just enjoying the moment.

Off in the distance, sailboats competed with fishing

boats

for the right spots to drift. Windsurfers rode with the

wind

while jet skis raced back and forth stirring the waters.

Paddle boarders stayed closer to shore avoiding the

swimmers who ventured beyond the sand bar.

I could go on and on, but you get the picture.
The varied activities produced a delightful view.

76 Cocaine

Fools beware,

this silent killer

dressed in white lace

slips incessantly into our land.

Countless dreamers

in search of utopia

daily fall victim

to her enticing promises.

But her highs

plummet faster than

the stock market crash,

leaving behind

the pleasure seekers

lost unto themselves.

So, fools beware

of this silent killer

dressed in white lace.

Her calling card,

etched in granite,

is no mirage.

For the wages of sin is death,

but the gift of God

is eternal life in Christ Jesus

our Lord.

Romans 6:23 NIV

77 A Different Kind of Christmas

Fortunes melted like snow in the spring,

piggy banks lost their flavor

that week in October of 2008.

As houses collapsed,

greed imploded upon itself

catching the world by surprise.

Giants fell like dominoes

taking with it innocent victims.

Like a runaway train,

all efforts failed to contain the bleeding.

It took a lot to bring the world

to the true meaning of Christmas.

But God knew if some were to be saved

the world must be brought down

to their knees and freed of their selfish desires

to have it all.

It was a different kind of Christmas that year.

I worshipped in a barn where
there were no cattle lowing
or donkeys braying softly,
Just an empty manger filled with straw,
and a spotlight focused on the empty cross.

Hymns of praise and thanks were sung
while weeping could be heard.
Those gathered knew the hope belonged
to those who held onto their Savior's Words.

"In the fullness of time God sent His Son...
"I am the bread of life,"
"I know the plans I have for you."
On and on, powerful words of hope were spoken.
"His Truth will get you through hard times and He
will be your peace.
Trust in Him, fill your minds with His promises and
He will dwell in your hearts," the Pastor said.
"All is not lost. Only the things of this world have an
end.
Remain in the Lord, and He will remain in You."

Quiet Amens could be heard as the service ended

and

the worshippers returned to their cars in darkness

filled with a renewed sense of God's loving care.

78 The Old Wicker Basket

I don't know about you, but I'm ready for winter to be over. The season has been way too long filled with wild storms and extremely cold temperatures. I need a few warm days to kick back and relax and let the summer sun melt my soul. A trip to the beach, an afternoon working in my flower garden, or reading a good book sitting on the porch swing would do the trick.

But I probably should write the family stories that continue to roam around in my mind and leave everything else to wait. The idea of organizing my thoughts and getting them down on paper is a little overwhelming, but also a good challenge.

Where to begin is the real puzzle. Maybe I'll start with my father, as the anniversary of his death isn't too far off. He was seventy-three years old when he died from bone cancer on June 29, 1982. It was a sad ending for such an active life.

Then there's my mother who lived another twenty-one years before she died at ninety-three. Her heart just gave out. Their experiences could have filled volumes with memories that I wasn't wise enough to capture on paper while they were still alive.

Much to my regret, my parents held several garage sales in their latter years, and many of the precious items I remembered as a child were sold.

When my mother downsized to an apartment, after my father's death, more treasures were lost forever. In her late eighties, she moved to a mobile home just a few miles from my house.

When she died, I discovered an old wicker basket in her closet filled with priceless treasures. Tucked inside were family pictures dating back into the eighteen hundreds. There were tin plates of fading faces, smiling couples printed on post cards and pictures of two uncles in a woman's broach. A scrapbook held dozens of yellowing photos of old homesteads, family reunions, and children playing. Many of the pictures have names recorded on them, people I never knew, but they are still part of my ancestry.

I foolishly allowed the immediate things in life to claim my time; missing the opportunity to record the history that belonged to these precious items my mother had preserved all these years. Sadly, their stories are lost forever.

Mother, also, had saved fourteen tall delicate crystal wine glasses belonging to my great-aunt Pearl. They are over ninety years old. I can envision my Aunt Pearl, dressed in one of her many elaborate outfits, drinking wine from these goblets while George Gershwin's Rhapsody in Blue drifts from her RCA Victor record spinning on the old phonograph. The records were among the garage sale casualties, but somehow, the wineglasses survived.

There were lockets, crosses, an old fountain pen, my grandfather's shaving mug, my mother's buttonhook for her shoes, and numerous other items. How my mother chose what to keep and what to give away is a mystery. Saving my great-grandmother's wedding skirt is understandable, but her old black cotton slip?

When I came across an old wrinkled paper bag, nothing could have prepared me for what it held. It was my father's christening gown. Dad had been baptized in the Catholic Church in the summer of 1909.

I often wonder what the church looked like in that small town of Continental, Ohio. Was it large and ornate, or was it a small, unobtrusive structure? And what was the weather like when my father was carried into the chapel dressed in this dainty beige gown? Was the sun shining or did it rain? What was the service like, and who held his tiny body as the water was sprinkled over his head and the lifesaving words were read? So many questions never asked, so much history gone forever.

I'm in awe as I handle his delicate little gown. Except for a few broken stitches, the garment is in excellent condition. There are no stains or tears in the fabric. Even the fine lace attached to the pin tucks on the bodice is still intact.

The dress is formed from fine batiste, finer than Egyptian cotton. Except for long puffy sleeves that are stitched by hand, machine made French seams hold most of the garment together. A tiny sleeveless underskirt and cap were also tucked in the bag. Of all the items Mother saved, this little gown is most cherished. It is an affirmation that one day my father and I will be reunited in heaven.

Before it is too late, I hope to have accepted the daunting task of writing the many stories about my family that I can still recall. Once completed, they will go to my children, and hopefully, they will be passed down to their children.

Reading a good book, sitting at the beach, or gardening will have to wait until I have fully embraced the discipline required to record our family's history.

Who knows, I may discover writing the stories delightful and definitely worth the time.

79 Simply Believe

There once was an orchard that had gotten

Left to itself, its fruit became rotten.

It was chopped all down,

Level to the ground,

And soon the trees were forgotten.

But the Gardener had plans for a tree,

Though it was known only to Thee.

A sprout burst forth,

From the stump, of course,

With time, it grew strong and free.

A storm appeared ravaging the tree,

Breakings it limbs for all to see.

Yet healing came,

By His powerful name,

And its fruit was sweet as could be.

For many the plan didn't make much sense.

The journey required was too intense.

Be willing to labor,

To love your neighbor,

Yet the wages were eternally immense.

Some ate the fruit and became wise indeed.

The secrets of life they did receive.

The old gave way,

To a new today,

And all they had to do was simply believe.

He (Jesus) said to them, "How foolish you are, and how

slow of heart

to believe all that the prophets have spoken!

Did not the Messiah have to suffer these things

and then enter his glory?"

Luke 24:25–26 NIV

80 The Bible

Why do I need it?
Why should I care?
It's only a book
that's not even rare.

> There're too many stories
> and chapters to find.
> There're too many words
> to confuse my mind.

Where would I start?
When would I begin?
I don't even know
the meaning of sin.

     * * *

> I thumb through the pages
> half-bored, I yawn.
> God speak to me now
> for it's almost dawn.

I laugh at the thought:
What if He does?
But surely, I'm not
one whom He loves.

> For my days have been filled
> with fast living, you see.
> My nights, seeking love
> have brought pleasure to me.

> * * *

I find myself reading
the words passing by
As I come to a section
that catches my eye.

> This person called Jesus
> speaks directly to me.
> "Repent! Be forgiven."
> "Come-follow me."

My face seems to flush;
My heart starts to pound;
I find myself weeping,
And kneeling down.

I hear myself say,

"I receive you as Lord.

Come into my life,

My soul be restored"

* * *

My days are more joyful

Since the battle He won.

But the struggles aren't over,

They've only begun.

So, I search His Word daily

To show me the way.

And He lovingly guides me

when I take time to pray.

* * *

If these are your questions

but you doubt that you're lost.

Just take my advice

It's free of all cost.

Don't challenge the Scripture

Just take it all in.

It's power-filled truths

Will purge you of sin.

For the Word holds great comfort

And hope for mankind,

But Satan is clever

In keeping you blind.

81 The Story Tellers

Who are these peoples who speak in different

tongues?

Where did they come from?

What is their purpose?

And who brought them together in this place?

They look like you, they look like me,

But they think oh so different.

Who taught them the wisdom that they share?

What schools did they attend?

Who are their teachers?

And how did they learn to state their case?

They look like you, they look like me,

Yet, their thoughts are always new.

Some speak of loss, some speak of love

And others just spin a tale

Of lives lived beyond the moon

And did they really travel to outer space?

They look like you, they look like me,

Except, I still don't understand.

The poet's message is oh so strong

Its cadence quick, your attention he holds

The message bold and to the point

Is often filled with kindness and grace.

They look like you, they look like me,

And I must admit, I beginning to see.

These storytellers retrace the steps

Of memories locked behind the gates

Their papers free the lives once lived

Creating visions like finely hand-woven lace.

They look like you, they look like me,

And they do it oh so well.

They look like you, they look like me,

Their gift from the Master with a story to tell.

82 The Broom Closet

In 1983, I created a clown ministry. The concept popped out of thin air. No prior planning had gone into the idea. The details simply evolved in a matter of weeks. It was amazing.

My birthday party clown had the most fun playing with children, but my favorite character was dubbed "The Crazy Lady."

She wore large blue tennis shoes with bright orange laces, bold colored striped knee-highs and long white bloomers trimmed with lace and red ribbon. A tight fitting short knit dress wrapped in large pastel stripes was embellished with gold drapery tassels at the hem while gaudy jewelry hung around her neck. Long white evening gloves added a touch of class along with her beautiful celery green boa and full-length tourmaline mink she often dragged on the floor. A large red smile that invited people into her world of joy covered most of her face. A crown of rainbow-colored curls topped off her outfit. She was a sight to behold.

As a speaker for churchwomen, diet groups, charities, and more, she carried a message that poked fun at life. Serious subjects were off limits because her goal was to leave her audience feeling uplifted and laughing. She did it so successfully that it almost seemed wrong to take money for having such fun.

Then one day, things changed. My mother secured a speaking engagement for me in her community. Once a year, the people from the surrounding area who once lived in Putman County, Ohio, held a picnic at her clubhouse, and this year, I would bring "The Crazy Lady" to entertainment them.

Mother and I worked for weeks putting together the script. When the day of the event arrived, people packed the hall. Lunch was served with helpings of laughter and excitement. I had been ushered into a small broom closet to make my transformation. A raw light bulb hung from the ceiling. An old wooden table and bench all but filled the cramped space.

I carefully covered my face with the white oil of the clown then added the final details. I slipped into my costume, said a prayer, and returned just in time to hear the president of the group introducing me.

Once again, laughter erupted. I wasn't quite what the group had expected, but the women applauded, even whistled. It took a few minutes for the men, who seemed a little uneasy, to accept me. Their tight lips and stiff backs soon relaxed as I began to describe events from the men's lives.

Eyes narrowed as they looked intently at me trying to figure out who I was, and how I knew so much about them. The mention of buying their first model A Fords, their amazement at watching the first airplane land near their hometown, and recalling the fun times dancing above the local general store—all brought waves of laughter into the hall. I delighted in seeing their faces light up when my stories touched their treasured memories. Everyone seemed to have a good time.

As I completed my dialog, I introduced myself and thanked them for being such good sports. I pointed out my mother and explained that it was she who had given me all their special memories. The people applauded her, and Mom glowed. Then to my surprise, the Spirit nudged me to explain about my father's absence.

"My father died a couple years ago," I said, "He was 73, and we sure do miss him. Cancer killed his earthly body, but as a Christian, I believe Christ has given him a new one, free of pain and suffering. He had been baptized and raised in a Christian church but stopped attending services after he and my mother were married. It was my privilege to lead my father into a personal relationship with Jesus a few months before he died. And it's my belief that one day we will be reunited in heaven."

I thanked them again for having me and returned to the broom closet. As I was removing my makeup, a soft tap, tap, tap came from the door.

"Come in," I said.

A tiny old lady entered the closet.

"Excuse me," she whispered. "I just want to thank you for sharing your joy with us, and especially the news about your father. You see I was one of his teachers at the school he attended. He was such a nice young man. I knew that he had left the faith," she continued. "It grieved me so. I prayed for him all these years and was delighted to learn that he had received Jesus as his personal savior before he passed. Thank you again," she said. Then she turned and disappeared out the door.

I was so dumbstruck, my head spun. She had known my father and in the midst of my bewilderment, I didn't even think to chase after her to learn more about their relationship. I had come to entertain a group of people as a silly clown. Yet God had sent me with a message to honor the prayers of this faithful little lady. I can still hear the joy in her voice and see the sparkle in her eyes. It was an unbelievable few moments filled with blessings far beyond my ability to record. And yet, each time I revisit that dusty little broom closet in my mind, God reveals another secret I had not seen before.

Edited & published in Women of the Secret Place
By Ruth Carmichael Ellinger and others. 2012
Ambassador International

83 And the Definition Is

Love comes in all colors, shapes and passions. It can demand all
of our senses. Love can be hard to describe. The precise meaning
of love is difficult to tie down as we use it so loosely.
Consider the following possibilities.

Love is: viewing a beautiful sunset on a cool evening,
seeing children playing happily together,
watching a killer storm miss your neighborhood,
opening your eyes and seeing for the first time,
gazing into the eyes of the one who holds your heart.

Love is: the laughter and conversations at the dinner table,
listening to the vows of the bride and groom,
the first cry of your newborn child,
receiving the news that you have won the lottery,

hearing the words, "I love you."

Love is: savoring a gourmet meal with a close friend,
biting into a piece of moist German chocolate cake,
enjoying an ice cream cone on a hot summer day,
sampling a glass of fine wine,
drinking a bottle of cold water in the desert.

Love is: coming home to the smell of fresh baked
bread,
experiencing the joy of walking through a garden of
gardenias,
catching the fragrance of your special perfume,
sensing the freshness of sheets dried in the outdoors,
the aroma of a steaming meal set before a homeless
person.

Love is: an extreme emotion of the heart,
the pride felt when a county's anthem is played,
the joy of experiencing your soldier returning from
battle,
walking in a gentle shower in the heat of summer,

the glue that holds a marriage together for fifty years.

I believe the most profound, perfect, ultimate
definition of love has
been given to all mankind from heaven in the
precious free gift
of Jesus Christ as one's Lord and Savior.

84 Mice in the Attic

Ring-a-ding ding, my smartphone did call.
The message commands
a life changing overhaul.
From uprooting my life, and a home of my own
to an apartment dweller with neighbors on loan.

Peaceful surroundings come crashing down
as the mice in the attic
come back into town.
They scamper up the stairs like an oncoming army.
The pounding of feet
destroys my harmony.

They clamor for order, the noise slows down,
out for the evening
to check out the town.
Aware of the change, I quickly retreat,
hopefully claiming

a good night's sleep.

The outcome uncertain, I hold my breath.

I'm here for the long haul,

outlasting the rest.

Finding the humor in each interruption

will add to my pleasure,

and relieve any tension.

So, I pray for the mice and all that they do,

for their peace of mind

their welfare too.

I want them happy and successful indeed,

so, they'll move out soon

I wish them Godspeed.

85 Texas Bound

One box, two, the packing began,
September came and went.

Cleaning the entire house alone
Allowed eyes to purge waiting piles.

Surprising finds of treasures lost,
October added her days.

Box fifty, fifty-one, the packing pushed on.
Overwhelmed, my body ached.

Russell's shed shared lawn tools
Followed by a Thanksgiving dinner.

Time out for family fun.
Needed rest came into play.

Box eighty-eight and nine,

Many December decorations curbside.

Garage tools left with friends

Playroom finished — unbelievable.

Getting closer, more boxes added

Last minute odds and ends disappear.

The end of January meets the goal

Box one hundred twenty-three wins.

The Moving Van arrives on February two.

Reality hits and butterflies appear.

Who would have believed

I had the strength to finish?

Only the Lord, for it was His doing.

The last three boxes left unnumbered.

Texas, here I come, ready or not.

To experience a journey of a lifetime.

86 Where to Now?

Twenty-two years of marriage cast aside by the pound of a gavel. There were two teenagers to care for, but how? Following my Air Force husband around the country for ten years left me little opportunity to create a career. Volunteering as a Boy Scout leader to teaching vacation Bible school didn't convey my real talent on a résumé for employment.

Therefore, I bounced around from being an office file clerk to working as a salesperson at a local clothing store.

Then, the theme song from Mahogany sung by Diana Ross appeared on the scene. Words like: *"Do you know where you're going to? Do you like the things that life is showing you, where are you going? Do you know?"* The words questioned my already confused mind.

"God help me," I cried. And He did.

Thus, appeared Russell Lafferty on the scene. My heart blinded my mind as I was drawn to him like a moth to a porch light. *"Do you get what you're hoping for?"* the song continues.

But what did I want? His personality proved to be controlling. I craved security. To my foolish heart, controlling and security seemed to complement each other. I had no idea where I was going.

As the song progresses: *"Once we were standing still in time, chasing the fantasies that filled our minds."* And that is how I felt when he embraced me, standing still in time. Love that only composers write about. "Where was I going?" I didn't care as long as I was with him.

A year and a half later we were married on Friday the 13th in October of 1978. We moved into our first house on April Fool's Day the following year. Our friends gave our marriage a maximum of three years.

"Your personalities don't fit for a successful marriage. It won't last," was their chant.

Did they know something I didn't know? Was I too close to the music that played in my head and in my heart? *"You knew how I loved you, but my spirit was free."*

Disney World proved to be one of our favorite playgrounds. Traveling around the country came in a close second. We both worked, we played well, but the everyday life ran into trouble. Arguing often-replaced laughter. Tears flowed as the tune played over and over in my head. *"Do you know where you're going to? Do you like the things that life is showing you?"*

I must admit, no matter how hard I tried, the answer was no.

Eventually the strong winds of life developed an inner strength in me, allowing insight into *"the fantasies that filled our minds,"* at least to those that danced to the music in mine.

The security I craved became a reality at a price. Most decisions were determined by what he knew to be true. Russell's legal mind left little room for the fantasies that roamed around in my world. All his efforts to change me seemed to fail, but that didn't keep him from trying over and over again.

"Why can't you be more logical?" he would demand.

"My brain isn't wired like yours," I would yell at him.

"Now looking back at all we've planned, we let so many dreams just slip through our hands." The question answered by the words of the song proved to be *no planning actually took place on our part.* The need to be loved by both of us overrode any logic, any planning, any thought of the future.

We lived in the moment of time like the first bloom of spring that brings such delight with no thought of the final outcome.

Almost thirty-three years of marriage proved our friends wrong. Sadly, cancer struck Russell and for his last two years, our fundamental differences slowly drifted away. Love, forgiveness, and gentleness filled our days.

The memories we created are stored on CDs, videos, and in the hidden chambers of my mind.

"Do you know where you are going?" the song ends. And what will tomorrow bring? I have no idea, but thank heaven; I do know I can trust the Lord with my future.

In their hearts humans plan their course,
but the Lord establishes their steps.
Proverbs 16:9 NIV

87 Celebrate Together

Come,

Walk with me

Through the ever-changing seasons of time.

In the spring,

Nature teaches us profound life lessons.

Using dried seeds,

She drops them into the open arms of the earth

Where sleep protects them until their time has come.

Then, slowly,

Almost magically,

The seeds begin to stretch —

Breaking out of their bondage —

Reaching for the light that beckons them upwards.

Finally, delicate, tender shoots

Peek through the ground,

Pressing towards the sunlight

That will fuel their growth,

Until their efforts are rewarded

With a harvest of lacy carrot tops.

Winding vines offer up green beans and peas,

Sturdy stocks of rhubarb and sweet corn

That promises a yield beyond belief.

Only a dreamer can vision such a wondrous display

Long before winter's snow is melted.

Summer, also, brings a myriad of gems.

There's the joy of

Dancing sea grass and plump wild grapes –

Warm waters that constantly kiss the waiting sand,

Waters that carry little boats to nowhere,

While thousands of individually sculptured shells

Await tiny hands seeking her treasures.

There is the joy of drinking in the splendor of

Sunsets and sunrises that is sharpened by summer
rains —
Rains that often turn tiny streams into flowing rivers
Where children swim unadorned
And fishermen gather to spin tales about the
"Big One"
That got away.

Rains that turn open fields into plush meadows
Where ball is played, picnics are eaten and peace
abounds,

Summer is more than generous with her offerings, as she
calls
Out to the child in each of us to slow down and enjoy the
moment.

Fall will not be outdone.

So, with cooler temperatures,
Her harvest of corn, wheat, apples, and gourds galore
Are gathered at fairs and festivals to be honored,

Before the soil begins preparation to sleep again.

Pumpkins put forth their best faces,

And the leaves of the forest wave their "Goodbyes,"

Having been splashed with brilliant colors

Of reds and orange, dotted with yellows and green,

Until they all seem to bleed together.

Her harvest rewards the efforts of the dreamers,

And her final celebration of the season

Always wins the blue ribbon.

As the warm air of fall passes on her baton,

Winter claims the spotlight,

And crystal-clear lakes, frozen in place, emerge.

Needles of ice cling precariously

As winter winds bite

Everything that gets in their way.

Her forests of tall stately evergreen trees,

Whose branches house the tiniest of creatures,

Are host to winter's best – snowflakes!

Millions of delicate ice crystals

Are welcomed

As they create flurries of bone chilling beauty.

Each etched individually,

Elaborate in design,

Come together as one

In piles deep,

Blanketing the earth

To keep the last bit of warmth contained

So, the soil can safely take her rest.

Such breathtaking beauty is freely given to those who dare
Accept her invitation to venture into her fierce elements.

So, come,

walk with me.

Together, we can celebrate the infinite beauty of the

seasons.

88 Change of Plans

Churning waters

Blustering winds

Hurried walkers

Before the storm comes in.

Stinging sand

Sunshine gone

The storm draws near

It won't be long.

Folding chairs

Grabbing things

Lightning strikes

The rain begins.

Plans for the day

Lying in the sun

All that changed

No time for fun.

Maybe tomorrow
Later today
Just have to wait
Before we can play.

Churning waters
Blustering wind
Scared off the beach lovers
They've all gone in.

89 Black Satin

Christmas season.
Time to let your hair down
and party in the country.
Friends gather, dinner served.

The lights dim, the music begins.
Slowly the couples embrace
moving to the rhythm of the melodies.
Then, in she walks,
tall, slender and on his arm.

Perfection from head to toe,
draped in glistening black satin.
Wearing a captivating smile.

Heads turn, whispers abound,
questions posed.
Who is this beauty he wears

like a badge of honor?

Where did he find her?
And why him?
He is nothing special.

He introduces her to a few of his associates.
Little details are shared before moving on.
The evening continues long into the night.

Before questions could be answered,
they disappear.
This mystery woman of the party
remains the secret of the man
who holds his cards close to his chest.

Merry Christmas everyone.

90 A Lady of Substance

A lady of substance

came walking by

my house one sunny day

        And by her side

        her faithful dog

        as red as Georgia clay.

I greeted her warmly,

 she spoke in turn

straight forward was her talk.

        Her name was Barb,

        a widow now.

        She lives just down the block.

As the days went by

we met again,

our friendship grew and grew.

        She swore a lot.

        That bothered me.

        I told her so she knew.

We visited often,

she taught me gin.

We loved playing cards.

We added two

to join the fun,

5-hand rummy, no discards.

Kings in the Corner,

Phase Ten too,

all was going well.

Then, cancer struck,

our focus changed

for Barb, only time would tell.

Love is needed

and laughter too,

if she this battle win.

The sharing of Jesus'

healing power

can only beat playing gin.

91 A Winner

Entertainment in the 1930s and 40s looked much different than today. The age of television had not arrived, and the average person had never heard of computers. My two sisters and I played on a swing attached to my mother's clothesline in the backyard. There was also a large sandbox our father made for us to play in. We also colored, played with paper dolls, and looked at comic books. For a nickel, we could walk to our local movie house. The distance challenged me, so I often stayed home. We had many friends, and life was near perfect.

Our father taught the three of us how to play checkers, penny poker, and several other board games. I loved sitting around the kitchen table, laughing as a family. For some reason, playing cards fascinated me the most. The process seemed to stir my sense of self-empowerment. I was in charge of my own hand, deciding which card to play and, once in a while, I even won a game. I was hooked at the age of seven.

As time passed, I learned to play Pinochle, Euchre, Hearts, Canasta, and several versions of Rummy. My love for the game continued throughout my life. When I retired, I formed a Thursday afternoon card club.

The group consisted of Barbara, who was a large, vocal, take-charge woman; Lorraine, a sweet bubbly blond who didn't have a negative bone in her body; Margaret, a sharp competitive game player; and me.

During the following months, as we played cards, we learned a lot about each other. Barb, as we called her, was a recent widow from Ft. Lauderdale. After her husband died, her daughter, Susan, insisted she move closer to her. So, Barb bought a house in Strawberry Ridge, fifteen minutes from her daughter.

Barb had a large red dog that was the love of her life. She was a unique woman who used profanity without blinking an eye. That bothered me, especially, when she'd take the Lord's name in vain. One day, I mustered up the courage and told her. I was surprised; she took it quite well and tried not to swear in front of me after that.

Lorraine came from Detroit, Michigan. She and her husband, Jim, had lived in Strawberry Ridge for¬¬ years. They had traveled all over the country in their RV after Jim retired from the police department. Lorraine said the funniest things and made us all laugh. Her cute little poodle loved the attention we showered upon her on the days we played cards at Lorraine's house.

Margaret had moved into the Ridge soon after Lorraine. She and her husband, Walter, came from New Jersey. They too had a cute little dog that barked a lot. Margaret loved playing cards, especially Phase Ten. She took playing cards very seriously, unlike the rest of us.

I was the youngest of the four with Ohio claiming my roots. My husband, Russell, and I were newcomers to the community. We didn't have a dog or a cat or even a bird. No time for pets, working and traveling kept us too busy.

Our backgrounds were quite different, yet we were very compatible. We chattered like teenage girls, laughing and sharing, making our time together special. Then, one day, Barb revealed that she had breast cancer. Actually, she had known about it since she had moved to the Ridge, but had decided not to take any action.

"I've had a long life," she told us, "and I don't want to end it going through chemo and being sick."

No matter how we tried to convince her, her answer was always *"NO!"*

"Seventy is young," we pleaded. "Breast cancer doesn't always kill you. Not anymore!"

"Sorry, I've made up my mind!"

Several months went by before her daughter, Susan, finally convinced her mother to go to a doctor. The diagnosis revealed the cancer had reached stage four. Barb still refused treatment. Susan was beside herself. Eventually she persuaded her mother to undergo chemotherapy, only to be disappointed again when Barb announced, *"No more chemo!"* In frustration, Susan resigned herself to her mother's wishes.

Weeks turned into months. She began cleaning her mother's house, buying her groceries, and maintaining her yard. Susan tried to balance the time at her job, with her husband, caring for her two children, and helping her mother. It was just too much for Susan. Her relationship with her mother became strained to the breaking point, so the visits became less and less. Denial seemed to set in regarding her mother's condition.

Therefore, Lorraine, Margaret, and I became Barb's main moral support. Then sadly, one day, Barb informed us she could no longer play cards.

"I'm just too tired. I've been fortunate to have experienced ample quality of life until now," she explained, "but unfortunately, the cancer has spread into my hip and the pain makes sitting for very long extremely difficult."

Hugs and tears ended our group. Lorraine and Jim helped Barb for weeks, until it became too much for them, so they passed the baton to me.

I visited Barb at least once a week. I made sure she ate. I often did her dishes. I even cleaned out her refrigerator. We always played several hands of Gin Rummy when I visited her. She usually beat me. She'd snap her cards down on the table and shout *"Gin!"* We'd both laugh.

Then, on Thursday, December 28, 2000, I walked down and fixed her lunch. She ate, we talked and after I washed the dishes, we played several hands of Gin Rummy. Nothing unusual, until Barb began to tell me about an experience in her past.

"I used to attend a Lutheran church long ago in New York. I even went to a Bible study on the book of Luke once. Surprised?" she asked, knowing I was a very active Christian.

"You're kidding me! I'm a Lutheran, too."

She beamed from ear to ear. Then, before I could finish my thoughts, she continued.

"I just couldn't buy the concept of grace, or the idea that Christ died for my sins. I wasn't that bad. The pastor told me one day I would accept the Lord's offer. I think today might be the day."

Unbeknownst to Barb, I had been praying for this moment for months. But her words caught me by surprise. I sat speechless for a moment. Then she began bombarding me with questions, questions she had been stockpiling for years. I tried my best to answer them, sharing Scripture as well as my faith.

"I struggled for years before I accepted the Word of God as Truth," I explained. "Each person's journey is different. One of my favorite verses is Mark 9:24. 'I do believe, (Jesus) help me overcome my unbelief.' This sentence helped me understand how receiving Christ into my heart didn't have to be connected to knowledge. Inviting Jesus into your heart just takes that leap of faith your pastor shared with you years ago."

We sat in silence. I could feel her wanting to let go and receive Jesus as her personal Savior. I clinched my teeth. I held my breath. I felt like I would explode.

Finally, in a quiet whisper, she said, "I guess it's time."

I gently took her hand in mine and praised God for His faithfulness in bringing her into His Kingdom, for waiting patiently for her to receive His Son. The electricity of the moment brought shivers to my spine.

Strangely, I had brought the email I had received that morning from a pastor friend, talking about the gift Christmas brings us each year. So, I read it to her.

"Christmas is a reminder of God's great love for each and every one of us," I read. "It's the gift of forgiveness and restoration, the hope and strength to navigate us through any set of circumstances. Isn't that a wonderful thought?"

"So, it's not a myth you can go to heaven," she questioned, ignoring my question, "even if you haven't lived a good life?

"Yes, Barbara, it's not a myth," I said. "Pastor also enclosed the words to a song he had recently heard entitled: 'This One's with Me.' I think the words are perfect for this moment, Barb. Let me read them to you."

"I was dreaming about heaven; dreamed I was standing at the pearly gates. We were all there, and I was so scared standing in the presence of one so great. I felt so very unworthy; I felt like running away. I bowed my head and I turned to go when I heard someone say: Father, this one's with Me, part of the family."

My voice broke and tears rushed into my eyes. I bit my tongue, but I couldn't go on so I repeated the words, "Father, this one's with Me, part of the family."

"Barb, Christ is waiting with open arms to usher you into heaven when you die."

We sat quietly for several moments just holding hands.

Finally, I gathered up my papers, put them aside, and suggested we play some more gin. She won every game. We both had a good laugh. I gave her a hug goodbye and walked home. Funny, I don't remember my feet ever touching the ground.

The following Tuesday morning I called her. "Have you had breakfast?" I asked.

"No, I'm not really hungry," Barb softly whispered.

"Well, stay put, I'm bringing some breakfast down to you."

I made a scrambled egg, half a toasted English muffin, half a banana, applesauce, and a small glass of milk. She played with her food, eating slowly like it was her last meal, and sadly, it was. She kicked over her water, spilled her milk, and could barely eat her eggs.

I became concerned as her head keep leaning to one side, so I called my neighbor who had been a nurse. She arrived in minutes and agreed with me that I needed to call 911. Next, we called her daughter, Susan.

Within fifteen minutes, Barb was on her way to the hospital. Susan followed in her car. At the hospital, the doctor put Barb on liquids, treating her for pain only. The cancer was taking its toll. Gravely ill, confused with pain, her lungs filling with fluid, Barbara sensed the beginning of the end had arrived. After running several tests, the doctor affirmed her suspicions. The cancer had spread throughout her entire body.

The next day, I got permission from Susan to visit Barb in spite of her being extremely weak.

"Hi friend, how are you doing?" I asked, placing a bouquet of red carnations on her table. They were her favorite.

"Oh, okay. I wonder why they arranged the flowers like that."

"Gosh, I don't know."

"What's that bottle of water over there on the wall? I should know, but I can't think."

The morphine had begun its mind-numbing process. We spoke for a few minutes. Then Barb's daughter asked me to leave. I took Barb's hand in mine, offered a short prayer, and kissed her cheek.

We smiled and I said, "Goodbye."

Susan called at 1:31 a.m., Sunday morning. "Mom is gone," she said. "It's over."

I lay in bed, praising God. It had been less than five days since Barbara took her leap of faith into the arms of her Lord. I feel so humble and privileged to have been a part of her journey.

I can still hear her snapping the cards down and shouting, *"Gin!"* Barbara would definitely tell you, if she could, that she finished her life *"a winner."*

92 Living Words

Write what you see,
The season, the song,
The color, the action,
That makes me go on.

See what you write,
The power, the flow,
Where does it take me
If I'm willing to go?

Write what words mean.
Is it cold to the bone?
Are you bent over laughing?
Will I hear the ocean foam?

Will I have a sense
Of an all-consuming fire,
Or the fragrance of a rose

That stirs my desire?

Will I feel your words touch me
Like the warm summer sun,
Or the chill of the winter
That's just barely begun?

Or are your words dull,
Flat on the page
Taking up space
Lacking of rage?

Oh, write what you see,
The noises you hear,
Please help me smell
Your sense of fear.

Express the action
In words that expand
My pleasure in reading
Your story in my hand.

93 Brain Drain

Teaching an old dog new tricks
in Texas surprised even me.

Portals, gate codes, passwords galore
all need to be memorized, recorded.

With the purchase of a Smartphone,
I am now up to date until tomorrow.

Technology changes faster than light.
My brain struggles to expand.

The day begins cold. By afternoon
it is hot. And wind, don't get me started
on that. How to dress is a puzzle.

Wait till summer I am told.

Traffic is limited, but one

must be watchful for deer migration.

In a split second they appear

claiming the right of away.

The most difficult obstacle yet

in the way of being settled is too

much stuff and too little space.

Time to eliminate more of my treasures.

Help me Lord to let go of them.

94 Believers, Be on Guard

The Accuser stands in the doorway
waiting patiently for his next conquest.
His quiver of lies ready to pierce
an unprotected heart.

Like a lion, he seeks to devour
An unsuspecting soul.
Who will be his next victim?
Who has forgotten to put on the armor of God?
Who has taken the covering of prayer too lightly?

Evil blankets our world.
It slips incessantly into our minds
allowing the darkness to corrupt our spirits.

Who will battle against this enemy?
What power can defeat this father of lies?

Where can one hide if not in the shadow

of the wings of our heavenly Father.

Be on guard believers, the wicked one brings death.

Yet, he is powerless against the Word.

Draw near to our God and be saved.

Jesus stands knocking at the door of your heart.

The LORD is near to all who call on him,

to all who call on him in truth.

He fulfills the desires of those who fear him;

he hears their cry and saves them.

Psalm 145:18–19 NIV

95 Curiosity Killed the Cat

<u>Curiosity</u>, *according to Webster, is the careful attention, the disposition to inquire into anything. To excite attention. Careful or anxious to learn; inquisitive (to seek by asking) fastidiousness = (difficult to please; delicate to a fault)* . . . Hummm! Doesn't sound like me.

My parents taught me to speak only when spoken to, especially at meal times. Children were to listen and not to be heard, at least not around adults, and never, never were we to question authority. Besides, it's been said that curiosity killed the cat, and I didn't want to be blamed for that. So, with that type of thinking, I did not cultivate much curiosity in me as a child.

As I grew older, my sisters appeared much smarter than me, so I hid my struggle to learn. My undetected dyslexia did not help matters. I learned to laugh when

295

I'd give a wrong answer, trying to hide my embarrassment.

Pride, eventually, filled my heart and so, I didn't ask questions in fear of appearing dumb. Because retention of information didn't come easily for me, I just decided, "Why ask?" I'll just forget whatever it is anyhow!

Fear dominated my thinking most of my early years. It wasn't until I met Christ in my thirties and surrendered to Him that I began to ask questions. And yet, confusion remained as I learned many questions have different answers, all of which are acceptable.

Society has suggested the rules I was taught are meant to be broken. Even researchers published conflicting truths. Now, publishers no longer require many of the rules of English, once taught as fact. What good are the questions: who, what, why, when, where, or how? Do they matter? Of course, they do! They stimulate thinking.

Each of us must find our own way in life, seeking our own truth. It is often hard work, but then, work and reward is what it is all about. Sharing part of our lives with others through the written word can bring joy and understanding, comfort and love, forgiveness and healing. So I read and study, write and question, laugh and share what God puts on my heart.

I'm still not very curious, although my mind is constantly busy. I'm seldom ever bored, as creativity continually triggers new thinking. Perhaps this is what could be called curiosity.

For me, life doesn't need to answer questions, unless there is a reason and even then, at the speed I think, I often forget what it was that I wanted to ask. It used to bother me, but I've made friends with my brain. If it wants me to be curious, it'll have to do the work.

96 In the Blink of an Eye

Lined faces linger on a wooden bench
Watching playful children giggling in glee
As they tumble among the leaves.

Several black wooly dogs circle a tree
Barking in response to the unending chatter of
squirrels
Safely perched in the treetop.

A carpet of colorful flowers dance in the wind.
Their petals of yellow and pink lace outlined in green
Kiss the passing butterflies.

A runner's feet slap the path as she whizzes by.
Skateboards follow, guided by laughing boys
Seemingly going nowhere fast.

Tiny handmade sailboats race across a pool of blue

As a father and son call out to the wind

encouraging their crafts into the winner's circle.

In the blink of an eye all these things

register in my brain and

I thank the Lord for eyes that can see.

97 Beach Talk

"I hear you are going to the beach."

"That's right."

"How wonderful."

"I think so."

"For an entire week?"

"Yes, seven full days."

"Are you going alone?"

"Just me and my laptop."

"Aren't you concerned?"

"About what?"

"Being all alone?"

"I live alone everyday."

"But this is different."

"I know, but the Lord will take care of me."

"I know too, but… I would be glad to come stay with you?"

"Thanks, but no thanks. I plan to rest, write and quiet my body."

"All alone?"

"Actually, I plan on spending some quality time with the Lord."

"What if I come down one day and we could have lunch?"

"That's sweet of you."

"I'm serious, concerning your age you shouldn't go alone."

"I won't be alone."

"Aha! You meeting a friend? Male?"

"You could say that."

"I knew it. I knew it. What's his name? Do I know him?"

"I think so. His name is Jesus Christ."

"Oh."

"I hope to work on being still, no television, no radio."

"That is serious down time."

"Yes, I'm not even going to go online, no email, no YouTube, no Google."

"Wow! Won't that be hard?"

"I supposed so."

"But what if you need to look up something for your writing?"

"I'll have my books I use."

"It seems you have covered everything, but I'm still going to pray for you."

"Thanks. I appreciate that"

"No real male friend, right?"

"I believe He's real."

"You know what I mean."

"See you when I get back."

"Bye."

"Bye."

98 Rose Petals

Entering my room

their sweet fragrance

greet me with your thoughtfulness.

Deep red, they stand ready

to express your heart.

Your eyes filled with desire

whisper longings beyond my expectation.

Time filled with laughter, joy and warmth,

country drives, silly shopping and meaningful

worship

turn the pages of time,

until

like the dance at our reunion,

the music eventually stopped,

and we went our separate ways.

But, I will remember forever,

with a thankful heart,

love offered,

but not to be

like the rose petals

gently floating from their place.

Their beauty spent, their purpose fulfilled,

their time had come and gone.

99 The Encounter

The evening sky was giving up her color as the members of St. John's Lutheran Church filed out of the sanctuary. The traditional Good Friday services had concluded in silence. My five-mile drive home continued peacefully until I turned the corner on the last stretch of highway leading to my apartment.

In a split second, everything changed. A small herd of deer leaped out of the woods next to the road, blocking the traffic. They zigzagged between the vehicles. Ten, perhaps twelve . . . I couldn't count them all as they traveled so fast. I slammed on the brakes. I sat stunned.

Unfortunately, one made contact with the front of my car. I could also hear others hitting the back of my trunk. I sat frozen, hands white; gripping the steering wheel while the deer leaning against my hood struggled to stay standing. Eventually, he collapsed onto the road. I could see him kicking and jerking.

"Lord, please don't let him die," I cried.

He never took his eyes off me and the iron horse that had felled him. It seemed like a lifetime till he lifted his traumatized body from the pavement. We continued to stare at each other.

Thankfully, the deer stood on all fours and appeared to be only shaken from his ordeal. Traffic began to move by us on my left. The deer didn't move, nor did I.

"What do I do, Lord? He doesn't seem to be hurt, but he won't get off the road!"

A man in the car ahead of me had stopped and watched the drama play out. When all the traffic cleared the scene, he exited his vehicle and, waving his hands, caught the deer's attention. With little effort, the animal bolted back into the woods and disappeared.

As this little town of Boerne explodes with growth, we are invading more and more of their territory. I pray this is my first and final highway encounter with these large beautiful creatures that call this Texas Hill Country home. Taking a deep breath, I released my brakes and headed to my apartment, where, checking my car, I found no damage had been inflicted. Tears welled up in my eyes.

It truly had been a Good Friday.

100 The Waiting Is Over

In the "Fullness of Time," the waiting had come to an
end.
The birth of the Messiah –
Long promised –
Had come to pass.

As the Son of God was delivered from Mary's womb,
Her appointed task was complete.

The "Truth" had been kept from the hearts and
minds of men
Until the God/man had reached the designated hour.

Then, "Love" drew men unto Himself –
Teaching, feeding and healing those in need.
And yet, much more would be required
For His assigned task to be complete.

His life on earth brought forth the victory
Prophesied in days of old.

His life – a journey to the cross –
Would pay the price for sin
And would come in droplets from the "Savior's"
veins,
Where forgiveness flowed into the "River of Life."

His "Love" opened the hearts of men,
And they were made new.

His "Grace" opened the eyes of men,
And they found peace beyond their understanding.

His "Truth" opened the minds of men
And they realized, the waiting God had provided,
was finally over.

Hear this – you who would listen –
The waiting was over when Christ descended into
hell –

Proclaiming victory over death –

Announcing the time had come

For all mankind to know that the "Fullness Of Time"

Was fulfilled in their hearing.

Know this – you who desire understanding –

The time of waiting is now behind those

Who look upon the "Hope" of God

For their salvation.

Know that the "Spirit" of all wisdom blows in the

wind

Filling the minds open to the "Truth."

Believe this – you who dare to surrender yourself

To the Christ called Jesus –

The time of "Promise" awaits your confession.

The season of fulfillment has come.

The time of joy of the "Redeemed" is within us!

Rejoice mankind! The waiting is over.

To Be Continued

ABOUT THE AUTHOR

Bette is a retired widow and a recent transplant from the Tampa Bay Area of Florida to Boerne, TX where she resides near her son and his family. She is a published author of life stories, Christian devotions, Bible Studies and skits. She is also an award-winning poet as a member of the National League of American Pen Women. Sharing the love of Jesus is her passion. You can contact Bette at bette.j.lafferty@gmail.com,

15281980R10200

Made in the USA
San Bernardino, CA
17 December 2018